The Mvengian Vision of Anthropological Pauperization

From the same author

Social stakes of Privatizations in Cameroon. Case of the Cameroon Development Corporation (CDC), Resource Publications, Eugene/OR, 2018, 149p.

Enjeux sociaux des privatisations au Cameroun: le cas de la 'Cameroon Development Corporation' (CDC), Paris, Edilivre, 2009, 157 p.

La vision mvengienne de la paupérisation anthropologique. Une piste de réflexion philosophique sur le ntù? Paris, Edilivre, 2011, 112 p.

The Role of the Congolese Catholic Church in Promoting Social and Economic Justice in Relation to Oil, Outskirts Press, Inc., Denver, Colorado, 2011, 133 p.

Paulin Poucouta, Le service de la parole de Dieu. Entretiens, Editions Paulines, Abidjan, 2016, 168 p.

The Mvengian Vision *of* Anthropological Pauperization

A Path for Philosophical Reflection on Ntù?

Hermann-Habib Kibangou

WIPF & STOCK · Eugene, Oregon

THE MVENGIAN VISION OF ANTHROPOLOGICAL PAUPERIZATION
A Path for Philosophical Reflection on Ntù?

Copyright © 2022 Hermann-Habib Kibangou. All rights reserved. Except for brief quotations in critical publications or reviews, no part of this book may be reproduced in any manner without prior written permission from the publisher. Write: Permissions, Wipf and Stock Publishers, 199 W. 8th Ave., Suite 3, Eugene, OR 97401.

Wipf & Stock
An Imprint of Wipf and Stock Publishers
199 W. 8th Ave., Suite 3
Eugene, OR 97401

www.wipfandstock.com

PAPERBACK ISBN: 978-1-6667-3709-7
HARDCOVER ISBN: 978-1-6667-9620-9
EBOOK ISBN: 978-1-6667-9621-6

September 7, 2022 9:09 AM

To my late father Adolphe BOUEYE,
To my mother Cécile,
To you my brothers and sisters,
Serge Patrick,
Michaëlle,
Roland Brice Ley,
Raïssa Cyrielle,
Christelle Marina.

To all those who,
by their advice, their actions
and their "ntùity", give me to think,
I dedicate this work.

"Only Africans themselves have the competence to judge what should be the form of thought they intend to institute. Judges of their own intellectual enterprises, they are also responsible for them, in front of their own conscience, in front of the communities of which they are part, but also in front of humanity as a whole, if it is true that each one, by working for the development of his own culture, thereby contributes to the determination of what the quality of man does."

—J. LADRIÈRE

Contents

Preface | ix
Acknowledgements | xi
Introduction | xiii

CHAPTER ONE
The Man, His Works and His Thought | 1

CHAPTER TWO
The Anthropological Pauperization of the Ntù | 22

CHAPTER THREE
Critique and Contribution of Anthropological Pauperization of the Ntù in African Philosophy | 39

CHAPTER FOUR
Mveng and His Heritage | 48

CHAPTER FIVE
The XXIst Century : A Century of Anthropological De-pauperization of the Ntù? | 55

CONCLUSION
A Pertinently Philosophical Question | 60

Epilogue | 64

Bibliography | 65

Index | 67

Preface

PHILOSOPHICAL PRODUCTION IN AFRICA must not betray the desires of the African people, nor disguise the reality of our continent. It must help our peoples to change their destiny into a desired one. To do this, we must ask ourselves how philosophy in Africa can have a real impact on African society.

Indeed, if there is an impact, it must be on three levels: social, individuality-collectivity and mentality levels. What does this mean?

African philosophy must be thought in view of solving problems specific to African society in particular, and to world problems in general. It must be a philosophy of liberation.

A philosophy that liberates our peoples from their multifaceted sufferings. This liberation will be more cultural. Culture is to be taken here in all its dimensions (political, social, economic, religious, anthropological, etc.). Philosophy must be a culture in Africa in order to have a real impact. In this regard, it must be part of the life of Africans. It is only in this way that it can give our people something to think about.

At the social level, philosophy should not be the problem of any one social group. It must be the problem that concerns the whole society, seeking to respond to the needs of this same society. This is where its social dimension lies.

Moreover, the African philosophy must call upon the African man, the ntù. In this regard, the latter must not be indifferent to philosophical production. So that, if every African is challenged

Preface

by this same philosophy, it will be all of Africa that will benefit from it. Just as they are concrete men caught in their individuality, who engage in philosophical research, and are challenged by problems specific to the African continent, just as this research must benefit African society (collectivity). This is the level of individuality-collectivity.

To these two dimensions is added another one: the mental dimension. A philosophy that does not have a real impact on mentalities, is a dead philosophy. So if African philosophy wants to survive, it must at all costs take into account all these criteria and perhaps even many others!

In focusing our attention on the production of science in Africa, we thought that, to a certain extent, many African thinkers respect in their writings the three criteria mentioned above. And no doubt Engelbert Mveng, is one of them, with his theory of anthropological pauperization.

Indeed, the mvengian vision of anthropological pauperization, cannot leave the ntù in an indifference that would make him / her unable to think for himself / herself. That is why, it seems to us - and we are convinced of it - that this anthropological pauperization challenges at a higher level, African society, at the same time as the ntù being in its vital dimension.

In its reflexive advance, and through it, anthropological pauperization ends up challenging the whole African society. In this regard, it is a path that leads somewhere, that is, towards an Africa that wants and can this time, take a good direction.

Acknowledgements

I THANK ESPECIALLY THE FACULTY of Philosophy St. Peter Canisius, for having led me in the meanders of the philosophical sofia (the wisdom of the love of wisdom).

I also thank all those who encouraged me to do this work. My companions of the novitiate: the late Francis Léopold Youmbi Ngaleu, Kisito Matrengar Nantoïallah, Samedi Joseph, Yves Djofang Kamga, Arsène Brice Bado, Paul Christian Kiti, the scholastics of the AOC (West African) Province and the ACE (Central African) Province. Thanks also to Hervé Ouattarra, Gervais Yamb, Fr. Ferdinand Muhigirwa, who read and corrected my imperfections.

A special thanks to Fr. Nzuzi Bibaki (big brother), who, in his "big brotherhood", and by accepting to direct this end of cycle work, advised, helped and encouraged me to finish it. May the love he has for Africa never dry up. Beyond his numerous occupations, may he be the "big brother" that he has always been, available and attentive to his little brothers.

Thanks to Gervine Ngoma for her encouragement and support.

Thanks also to Michaëlle Boueyi and Célestin Kouma for re-typing the word version of the manuscript, from a PDF copy, the original version being lost.

Thanks to Godwill Ghenghan, Hélène Nguemgaing, William Mbilinyi, Bryan Manning and Augustin Koffi for their comments and suggestions.

Thanks also to Ousmane Touré, Divinat Malonga and Guy Savi who helped me find certain documents essential to this research.

Finally, thanks to Christelle Marina for sending the computerized data.

Introduction

How to Philosophize Differently?

IN THE PAST, speaking of African philosophy was considered by some thinkers, especially "Europeans"—believing they had a monopoly on this very demanding enterprise of philosophizing—as a linguistic abuse.

Today, to ask whether or not there is an African philosophy, corresponds more or less to "digging up" a question whose only clue to its existence would only show us its skeleton, as if to signify that it has indeed existed in history, but that it has gone away for good. Still, it is necessary that the diggers have not passed, for "ends" (from the Latin 'finis' that is to say goals), other, known only to them.

The story of whether or not there is an African philosophy is therefore an old-fashioned story. And the question of whether there is, or not, an African philosophy is a defunct question. It is up to African men and women who want to embark on this adventure that links reason to truth, that is, those who want to marry with thinking, to know what they are looking for. Africa needs such thinkers. And undoubtedly, these thinkers already there or to come must have the good will for the noble work which is theirs and be men and women of a non-doubtful competence. Their thoughts and know-how must be put at the service of Africa and of all humanity. They must have a deep and abiding love for Africa so that those who come after them will not question their know-how and their commitment to the socio-economic, political, scientific,

Introduction

cultural, religious, theological and philosophical development of Africa and in Africa. This is the price of their contributions. Such an undertaking is demanding and:

> We must say to the generations that are opening up to research: arm yourselves with science to the teeth and go and snatch, without mercy, from the hands of the "usurpers" the cultural property of Africa of which we have been so long frustrated: These scholars have not been worthy because they have taught untruths and have fallen back to the rank of vulgar ideologues who, under an apparent scientific serenity, are rabidly engaged in cultural aggression... The conditions for a true scientific dialogue do not yet exist in the so delicate field of human sciences, between Europe and Africa. In the meantime, African specialists must take conservative measures. It is a question of being able to discover a scientific truth by one's own means, without the approval of others, to know how to preserve one's intellectual autonomy... The era of deception, of intellectual swindling is definitively over... Competence becomes the supreme virtue of the African who wants to de-alienate his people... An action can only be revolutionary insofar as it is deeply rooted in the history and the national culture. (Cheikh Anta Diop 1973, IX-X).

In this book, we pay particular attention to a son of Africa who opened up to reflection, research and "armed himself with science to the teeth", to restore to Africa—without complacency or false modesty—its true image: Engelbert Mveng.

Our approach, which focuses solely on his theory of anthropological pauperization, can be in our humble opinion—and probably is—, a path for philosophical reflection on the ntù.

> The term "ntù" is the first of the "proto-bantu" language, an imaginary language that African linguistics is reconstructing as the basis of all "ntù" languages. Its existence is confirmed by the fact that several terms in these languages are similar or have the same roots (...) The term "ntù" (man) thus refers to the race of the "Bantu" of Black Africa. (Nzuzi Bibaki 1993: 76 footnote).

Introduction

As a little philosophical as it may appear, in the eyes of those who are allergic to the non-use of the philosophical language game, anthropological pauperization is a reflection of the African man, of the ntù, on his being-there and on his becoming.

First of all, it is an existential ethics because it characterizes the realization of a man's moral behaviour in his unique individuality (Rahner 1965: 160).

Then, a personal ethics so that it characterizes the immediate lived of the concrete experience (Rahner 1965: 160) of the ntù.

Therefore, reflecting on the ntù is a philosophical question if philosophy is this questioning, this reflection that one carries on the questions of concrete existence and experience, of man, of the ntù. This reflection, this questioning, encompasses the conception of man, the ntù, his vision of the world, his religious, political, social, anthropological, sociological, cultural conception, etc. And like Engelbert Mveng said, "a man who feels the need to reflect on major problems of human existence makes philosophy" (Mveng and Lipawing 1996: 45). He is aware of this and knows it. He is not, as Fabien Eboussi Boulaga would say, the "Mr. Jourdain of philosophy" (F. Eboussi Boulaga 1968: 5).

There is not only one philosophy, there are philosophies. And all are different from each other: so we talk about the philosophy of Eboussi, that of Tshiamalenga, the philosophy of Obenga or that of Hountondji, etc.

Difference is therefore what characterizes one philosophy compared to another. Finally comes the problem raised: the problematic. It emerges from the plan we have proposed to follow.

Just as the problematic raised by African philosophy is not the same as that raised by another philosophy, so African philosophy is different from European, Asian, Oceanic or American philosophy. African philosophy is not the one found in the manuals of philosophy typical of such a country. Nor is it the philosophy of Descartes, Kant or Heidegger. "From there, to say that, because they (these manuals) do not correspond to (European) book models, Africans do ethnophilosophy or ethnotheology, is to show a lack of culture." (Mveng and Lipawing 1996: 46).

Introduction

Making Europe the only legitimate reference in philosophical or scientific production, while thinking, questioning, reflecting, are not the prerogative of a single people, is probably an imperialist illusion.

The danger of such an exclusivist way of conceiving things is to look like an extra-terrestrial, someone who would no longer have his feet on the ground, but who would then have to be brought back to earth. Doesn't philosophy have to question our life here on earth with all the problems that (African) man, the ntù, has to face, and which at the same time, are intrinsic to this same life? African philosophy must start from the lived experience, from our lived experience. It is not a question of banal problems, but of existential ethics and personal ethics.

The plan of this book is as follows: an introduction followed by a first chapter that is devoted to the presentation of the author, some of his works, and the presentation of his thought. What does it mean?

It is about a biography, some of the author's excerpts on anthropological pauperization. And this, through some works by the author, the angle from which Engelbert Mveng addresses this anthropological pauperization as well as the main idea that seems to emerge from each selected work. This brief journey goes without a certain search for the first emergence of this concept in the writings of its author. A commentary and an allusion to the other works of its author put an end to this first chapter.

The second chapter focuses on the anthropological pauperization of the ntù: what Engelbert Mveng thinks of it, the embarrassment of the ntù who is in this situation, and the different types of this anthropological pauperization.

The third chapter deals with the criticism and contribution of the anthropological pauperization of the ntù in African philosophy. It is about seeing the limits that such a vision can have, the stakes of the problem posed and the challenges it raises. The fourth chapter is an excerpt from a lecture we gave during our philosophical studies at St. Peter Canisius Faculty of Philosophy in Kimwenza (Kinshasa/DR Congo). These first Mveng days (1997–1998) were

Introduction

an initiative of young Jesuits from the West African Province (AOC). The last chapter is a meditative reflection on what the 21st century could be for Africans. Finally, a conclusion will necessarily lead us to put an end to this work.

In a word, we propose in this book to study, analyze, question, understand and criticize the theory of anthropological pauperization as developed by Professor Engelbert Mveng, a Cameroonian Jesuit who was assassinated during the night of April 22–23, 1995 in his residence in Nkol Afeme, a few kilometers from Yaoundé.

CHAPTER ONE

The Man, His Works and His Thought

> This first chapter briefly presents Mveng, his work and his thought. Concretly, it is about some biographical elements, three of his work related to anthropological pauperization, the question inherent in Mveng's use for the first time of this notion of anthropological pauperization, a commentary on this same concept and a word on his other writings.

ENGELBERT MVENG IS AN EMBLEMATIC and prophetic figure, well known in the African religious and intellectual world. His immense work has gone beyond the borders of our continent, to such an extent that some could not help writing about him:

> The professional of language,
> the artist of the word,
> the interpreter of the African symbol
> who became a symbol himself (...).
> One of the most famous sons of this Africa
> of which he contributed to the international influence,
> The man citizen of the world,
> a leading figure in the history of modern times.
> Reverend Father Engelbert Mveng is no more.
> This soft and percussive voice,

The Mvengian Vision of Anthropological Pauperization

sober and prolix, voice of which one never tired of listening to the learned and incisive accent...[1]

These few words can indeed summarize what the man was. African, Cameroonian, theologian, Jesuit priest, historian, poet, musicologist, artist, sculptor, liturgist, archaeologist, anthropologist and philosopher at the same time. In short, a great thinker.

All truly great men, said Lachelier,[2] were original, but they did not want or believe they were on the contrary, it was by seeking to make their words and deeds, the appropriate expression of reason that they found the particular form in which they were destinated to express it.[3]

Biography

Of Cameroonian nationality, Engelbert Mveng was born on May 9, 1930 in Enam-Nkal of Minlaba, in the southern part of Cameroon, more precisely in the diocese of Ebolowa. Son of Jean Amougou and Barbe Ntolo, Engelbert Mveng received a Christian education from an early age. Baptized on July 14, 1935, and confirmed on July 28, 1942, Mveng was admitted to the Minor Seminary of Efok in 1944. In 1945, he left the Minor Seminary of Efok to continue his secondary studies (from the fifth to the first grade) at the Minor Seminary of Akono (Yaoundé); this, until 1950. Firm in his desire to become a priest, young Engelbert was sent on probation, during which he taught Greek, Latin, music, drawing and Ewondo in fifth grade. After a year of philosophy at the Major Seminary of Otele, Yaoundé (Seminary in which he had to finish at the same time his secondary studies), Mveng, wishing to become a Jesuit, was admitted (at the age of twenty-one) to the novitiate of the Society

---

1. L'Effort camerounais 22 (1019), Editorial *"Père, pardonne-leur car ils ne savent pas ce qu'ils font!"* In L'Effort camerounais from April 28 to May 12, 1995. This is a Bilingual Catholic bi-monthly news magazine from Cameroon. Property of the Episcopal Conference.

2. Lachelier (1832–1918), was a French idealist philosopher and critic.

3. Gusdorf, *Pourquoi des philosophes?*, 196.

The Man, His Works and His Thought

of Jesus in the province of Central Africa in Djuma (Kwilu) in the former Belgian Congo (ex-Zaïre) today Democratic Republic of the Congo. It was on September 29, 1951. On September 22, 1953, he took his first vows. De facto, he is the first Cameroonian Jesuit. Then, he left for Namur (Belgium) to study literature (1953–1956), continued philosophy (for a year) in the Jesuit scholasticate of Eegenhoven (Louvain), and finished it in Vals-près-le-Puy (France) in 1957. From 1958 to 1959, Engelbert Mveng taught history and French (in third and first grades) as regent (trainee) at Libermann College in Douala (Cameroon). From 1960 to 1963, he studied theology at Fourvière (Lyon), in France. On September 7, 1963, in Lyon, Mveng was ordained a priest of the Society of Jesus.

One day in 1964, he received the Broquette-Gonin prize and was promised Laureate of the French Academy for his book entitled, *Histoire du Cameroun* (1963). That day, the newspaper *Le Monde* paid him a beautiful tribute. Back home in 1965 he devoted himself to university teaching. As a great connoisseur of Greek and Latin languages, poets and ancient historians, he taught ancient history. In 1970, Mveng defended his thesis in History *Les sources grecques de l'histoire négro-africaine, depuis Homère jusqu'à Strabon* (Paris-Sorbonne), under the supervision of Professor Henri Van Effenterre.

For 30 years, from 1965 to 1995 (the year of his assassination), he taught history at the University of Yaoundé, joining several apostolates at the same time. Here, he was a student chaplain, there founder-director of a Negro art workshop, here founder (in 1980) of the female branch of the Congregation of the Beatitudes, and of the male branch in 1986, there secretary. Engelbert Mveng was, among others, secretary of MICA (Movement of African Catholic Intellectuals created in 1970), secretary of AOTA (Ecumenical Association of African Theologians created in 1977), head of the National Commission for Ecclesiastical History of Cameroon, head of Cameroon's national pilgrimage office (with pilgrimages organized to Rome, Jerusalem and Lourdes), UNESCO expert consultant, founder of African history library in Yaoundé, Negro art museum (Alioune Diop Museum) since 1980, and member of various African culture committees.

Engelbert Mveng was also a member of the Overseas Academy, a member of the Technical Committee for the preparation and general rapporteur of the first Negro Arts Festival (Dakar 1966),[4] during which he befriended another monument of African culture, Léopold Sédar Senghor. He was also for eight (8) years, Director of Cultural Affairs of the Federal Republic of Cameroon (a position equivalent today to that of Minister of Culture), head of the Department of History at the University of Yaoundé from 1983 to 1986, and vice-president of the Union of Black World Writers.

In addition, Engelbert Mveng did archaeological research at the sites of Ngoro (1966), Mimetala (1968), Mvolyé and Obobogo in Cameroon.

In 1972, he left St Francis Xavier community in Yaounde to live in town. In 1974, he stayed at the Foyer Jeanne Amougou (named after his older sister) that he had just created. In 1975, Engelbert Mveng founded a private and non-denominational college, *Le Sillon* (to which he will give the name of his older sister Jeanne Amougou who died shortly before). For the proper functioning of his college, he will call on eminent university professors.

As far as inculturation is concerned, he was very involved. First, in the inculturation of the liturgy, in the making of certain religious vestments, then in the center he created in 1992 : CARI (African Center for Research on Inculturation).

Engelbert Mveng has made high-quality works of art, including one in Yaounde Cathedral, another in the chapel of the Jesuit Theologate Hekima College in Nairobi (Kenya), and another in the Church of the Holy Angels, a parish (much frequented by Blacks) in Chicago in the USA in 1990. "At the inauguration of this church, he was given an envelope that he refused with great dignity to the astonishment of all. Proudly he said, "I gave them a testimony of

---

4. The Third Festival of Black Arts was held in Dakar from 10 to 31 December 2010.

The Man, His Works and His Thought

the sense of gratuity and nobility of heart of the black Africans. Their art cannot be exchanged".[5]

Engelbert Mveng is the author of several works[6] on African history and archaeology, a collection of poems (Balafon), monographs of art and poetry, various textbooks on the history of Cameroon. Three of his works "have made a significant contribution to the development of African culture" (Jesuits 1974–1975: 168), namely the Pan-African Cultural File (Paris 1966), the Cultural Message of Africa to the modern world (Addis Ababa 1966) and the Bibliographic Guide of the Black World (Yaoundé 1971).

Mveng was an exceptional man, with multiple qualities. "A man overflowing with activities, with provocative and stimulating writings and speeches."[7] Therefore, Father Peter Hans Kolvenbach, then General Superior of the Jesuits, could not help but write in a letter:

> The figure of Father Mveng is destined not to be erased from the memories of those who knew him closely, nor from the memory of all his confreres in the Society of Jesus. The rich personality of Father Mveng made him a Jesuit with remarkable qualities whose reputation had long since crossed the borders of Cameroon and even those of the African continent. Known and internationally recognized, he has distinguished himself both as a historian, as a university lecturer and as an apostle all committed in a pastoral care of intellectuals. It is also important to mention his remarkable artistic qualities, which allowed him to produce works of real value, and especially the deep conviction with which had devoted himself to the cause of inculturation of the faith in Africa.[8]

---

5. Bibaki, *Sango Ya Kimwenza*, 10.

6. Yvon Christian Elenga, "Engelbert Mveng : une lecture africaine de la Bible." Hekima College 19 (1998) 91–104. See also Paulin Poucouta, "Engelbert Mveng: une lecture africaine de la Bible." Nouvelle Revue Théologique 102 (1998) 32–45.

7. Renard, *Nouvelles de la PAO*, 3.

8. Kolvenbach, *Nouvelles de la PAO*, 2.

As a researcher, artist and African thinker, Engelbert Mveng travelled a lot, and gave conferences around the world.

But what about Mvengian thought ? It seems that three axes and a specific angle of approach can be drawn in Mvengian thought. First the cultural axis, then the historical axis, and finally the theology-spirituality axis.

The cultural axis is perceived in Mveng as the foundation, the very root of everything. This axis conceals indeed, the specific conception of the black man and woman, of the ntù, on Man, the world and the Beyond/God.

> Culture is first and foremost the conception of the world, of God, proper to a given people and from which these peoples try to organize their daily life , to organize the world in which they live and to organize their own system of thought.[9]

The historical axis consists in Mveng, firstly, to restore the truth on Africa, secondly, it is a history of civilizations; thirdly, it is the history of the people of Africa in their diversities; fourthly, it is the religious history of the countries of Africa.

> Our major concern is first to reconstitute the truth about the presence of our peoples in history at all times in the past. (. . .) The history that we write, the one that I write, is a history of civilizations. In this way, the contribution of our peoples to the transformation of the world and to the development of humanity is what most interests us. (. . .) The history that I write is also the history of our peoples in their diversities and in the fundamental unity of their historical destiny . . . Finally, I write, among my historical research, the religious history of our countries, in particular, the history of Christianity.[10]

The theology-spirituality axis occupies in the mvengian thought a non-less important place. It is essentially here, the African theology of liberation which according to Engelbert Mveng

---

9. Mveng and Lipawing, *Théologie, Libération et Cultures africaines*, 58.
10. Mveng and Lipawing, *Théologie, Libération et Cultures africaines*, 80.

was born in Africa. This African theology of liberation encourages an African reading of the Bible.[11] Engelbert Mveng, who at the same time takes advantage of having recourse to African traditions, understands spirituality as "the knowledge that man has of God through his religious experience."[12]

All these three axes can be approached more from one specific angle, which is the liberation of Black men and women. Beyond the liberation of Black men and women , there is the liberation of all humanity.

Presentation of some extracts of the writings inherent to the anthropological pauperization

This section is a presentation of a few works in which the concept of anthropological pauperization is analyzed. The goal is to identify this concept closely to see the reality it concretely translates, and highlight the issue of the problem posed by Mveng.

We are no longer unaware that the concept of anthropological pauperization surrounds the African, the ntù, in a problematic situation. This position cannot leave indifferent any African "who is not victim of not daring to think."[13]

We have selected the following writings for our reflection:

a. "Paupérisation et développement en Afrique."[14] In Terroirs, n° 01 May 1992: 111–119.

b. L'Afrique dans l'Eglise. Paroles d'un croyant.[15] Paris: l'Harmattan, 1987, 228p.

c. In collaboration with Benjamin Lipawing, Théologie, Libération et Cultures Africaines. Dialogue sur l'anthropologie

---

11. Mveng and Lipawing, Théologie, Libération et Cultures africaines, 28–29; Mveng, Spiritualité et libération en Afrique, 14 ; Poucouta, "Engelbert Mveng : une lecture africaine de la Bible," 32–45.

12. Mveng and Lipawing, Théologie, Libération et Cultures africaines, 23.

13. Eboussi, "Nous sommes victimes de ne pas oser penser", 22–23.

14. Pauperization and Development in Africa.

15. Africa in the Church. Words of a believer.

négro-africaine.[16] Yaoundé-Paris: Clé-Présence Africaine, 1996, 232p.

"Paupérisation et développement en Afrique"

This is an article published in the periodical Terroirs (founded by Fabien Eboussi Boulaga).

In this article, Engelbert Mveng points out, "President Ronald REAGAN, bidding farewell to the United States after his two terms in office, declared to the world that the United States economy had never been so prosperous. At the same time, all over Africa and the Third World, the cry of despair of countless peoples crushed by a blind, insatiable, relentless economic crisis, unleashed like a pack of rabid dogs on our starving peoples, has been rising for nearly three years."[17]

We are, as these words tell us, in front of two worlds, the first of which is rich and gets richer by making the other poor, and the second poor, impoverished by the wealth of the first. What a paradox!

Still according to Engelbert Mveng, "poverty reveals, in an undisguised way, the deep structure of contemporary human society in relation to material goods. This structure is based on iniquity and excess. It is unfortunately a truth which does not honor humanity: the totality of the wealth of our planet is controlled by a handful of men who represent hardly 20% of the population of the globe, the remaining 80% live in misery."[18]

Worse still, "it is in the rich countries that we talk the most about poverty" while in Africa, little is written about poverty, if not about development or underdevelopment. This observation leads Engelbert Mveng to read poverty in rich countries and in impoverished countries. He notes that:

---

16. Theology, Liberation and African Cultures. Dialogue on Black African Anthropology.

17. Mveng, "Paupérisation et développement en Afrique," 111.

18. Mveng, "Paupérisation et développement en Afrique," 112.

Poverty, in these countries of abundance, is first of all a tare that strikes individuals, families, or a certain social class. It is essentially a deprivation and exclusion, deprivation of material goods considered necessary or useful by the affluent society in which one lives; exclusion of social and cultural advantages which are the prerogative of the average man within the same society.[19]

But this phenomenon, thinks Engelbert Mveng, is linked to a certain number of factors of which:

a. The accumulation of material goods and enrichment as the norm of the economic life of society and the state;

b. The recognition of the fundamental rights of the human person and a certain freedom of enterprise;

c. The injustice and inequality in the distribution of goods;

d. The real sovereignty and power of the state;

e. A collective awareness of social inequity and a certain implementation of appropriate means to remedy it.

In Black Africa on the other hand and in the countries of the Third World, continues Engelbert Mveng, "poverty affects, in the first place, the institutions and the structures."[20] The first victim of this poverty, is the African State which, "as of its accession to independence, is deprived of the attributes of the true sovereignty."[21] Because, "by becoming independent, the African people were taken in the unpreparedness. Not only they were not asked for their opinion on the model of State that they wanted to give to themselves, but also their political leaders fought more for power,—their power,—than for the liberation of their people."[22]

In this sense, the State appears as an instrument of annihilation of the people. It is, from its origins, dangerous because it does not allow the people to enjoy favorably their freedom. It is a State

---

19. Mveng, "Paupérisation et développement en Afrique," 113.
20. Mveng, "Paupérisation et développement en Afrique," 114.
21. Mveng, "Paupérisation et développement en Afrique," 114.
22. Mveng, "Paupérisation et développement en Afrique," 114.

that acts more by force than by reason. The reason for its strength is thus: resignation, dispossession of oneself, etc.

> The African State, from its birth, is an instrument of domination, oppression, exploitation of the people, which has passed from the hands of the colonizer to the hands of the African political leaders. This instrument is all the more effective because it is an apparatus of pauperization whose mechanisms are based on two principles:
> a) deprivation of the instruments of sovereignty;
> b) and weaving a subsistence system based on absolute dependence.[23]

This is explained by the fact that the State is confronted from its origin with very precise problems that cannot be neglected: money is the first of them, followed by the lack of a proper monetary system, the lack of a military power worthy of the name. The armies are "trained and supervised by foreign powers; their often obsolete weapons are supplied and controlled by the same powers."[24] This fact is moreover deplorable for the simple reason that the African State is then established without an economic sovereignty. Everything that concerns the sale of export materials is imposed on it from outside, without its opinion. At best, if its opinion is requested, it is not up to it to decide, but only to fulfill formalities.

For its survival, the African state is condemned to beg politically, economically, financially, etc.

In "Paupérisation et développement en Afrique," Engelbert Mveng mentions anthropological pauperization explicitly. Here, he defines pauperization as "the act of becoming or making poor." This definition of pauperization is based, as said above, on Mveng's reading of the post-colonial African state, and by implication, on that of the black man, that is to say, the ntù.

In fact, according to Engelbert Mveng, anthropological pauperization is present at five levels, which we will present and

---

23. Mveng, "Paupérisation et développement en Afrique," 114.
24. Mveng, "Paupérisation et développement en Afrique," 114.

analyze further in the second part of our reflection. These five levels or types of anthropological pauperization are: structural pauperization, pseudo-philanthropic pauperization, corruptive pauperization, indebtedness pauperization and cultural pauperization. All these pauperizations hit the ntù in his everyday life, and this for decades.

However, even if Engelbert Mveng spoke about the anthropological pauperization by basing himself on the figure of the State, it appears that it is the Black man and thus consequently, the ntù who is threatened in his life. The State is to be understood here as an institution. But behind the institution, there are men who live and who, in spite of the hard reality of life, try to make the State function, even if those who direct them, behave as oppressors.

Before listing the different uses of the concept of anthropological pauperization, we note that in "Paupérisation et développement en Afrique," Engelbert Mveng approaches pauperization from a sociological, anthropological, political and even historical perspective. The anthropological, political and historical angles are given a large place, while the sociological and religious angles are given very little space.

Let us now list the different sentences of this article, inherent to the understanding of pauperization:

1. The African State, from its birth, is an instrument of domination, oppression, exploitation of the people, which has passed from the hands of the colonizer to the hands of African political leaders. This instrument is all the more effective because it is an apparatus of anthropological pauperization.[25]

    Here, the angle approached by Mveng is political, historical, and anthropological.

2. Pauperization. If we understand by pauperization the fact of becoming or of making poor, it is necessary to stop for

---

25. Mveng, "Paupérisation et développement en Afrique," 114.

a moment on the approach that we have just tackled on the African State.[26]

The angle here is much more historical than political or anthropological.

3. We have seen that poverty, at this level, affects the very essence of the State, in its political, economic, military, financial and ideological dimensions. Insofar as such a State begs for its subsistence from one of the foreign Powers, these Powers have the choice between two attitudes. Either to abolish the different forms of indigence that affect the beggar State in its essence, and thus restore its total sovereignty, (history does not present us with any such examples, nowadays, in the Third World); or to perpetuate, by subtle mechanisms, this multiple indigence and the bonds of dependence that it weaves between the beggar State and the Good-Samaritan State. The latter can then resort to mechanisms of pauperization that tend to maintain the status quo between it and its client.[27]

The reference to politics, history and religion is obvious.

4. Pauperization can thus be situated on five levels:[28]

- structural pauperization;
- pseudo-philanthropic pauperization;
- corruptive pauperization;
- pauperization of indebtedness;
- and finally, cultural pauperization.

This sentence is approached from a properly political angle.

---

26. Mveng, "Paupérisation et développement en Afrique," 115.
27. Mveng, "Paupérisation et développement en Afrique," 115.
28. Mveng, "Paupérisation et développement en Afrique," 115–116.

The Man, His Works and His Thought

We will go deeper into the content of all these different pauperizations in the second part of our reflection. If there is one main idea in this article, it is that of liberating and rehabilitating the black man in all his dignity.

L'Afrique dans l'Eglise. Paroles d'un croyant (1985)

In this book, Fr. Mveng reserves some pages to the anthropological pauperization. In this work, the idea of anthropological pauperization is manifest in the following angles: political, historical, economic, sociological, religious, economic, etc.

Here are the different uses:

1. From the end of the Middle Ages to present day, the history of Africa has known two dramatic stages: the slave trade and colonization leading to independence. The slave trade represents our anthropological annihilation . . . it is the pure and simple negation of our humanity.[29]

    The most influential angle of this sentence is the historical angle.

2. Colonization is basically a new form of exploitation in which the Negro will be used, no longer in the plantations of America, but in those of his own country. On this point, the whole of Europe is unanimous. Africa, an immense reservoir of free and docile labor, had just entered its phase of anthropological pauperization.[30]

    The political and historical angles are evident in this sentence.

3. That the Black Race, on the map of the world, in North America, Latin America, South Africa and elsewhere, solely because of the color of its skin, should be annihilated in its human dignity and stripped of all human rights, this is

---

29. Mveng, *L'Afrique dans l'Eglise*, 203.
30. Mveng, *L'Afrique dans l'Eglise*, 205.

The Mvengian Vision of Anthropological Pauperization

the great racial ideology of the colonial powers, even when it is verbally condemned. The destiny of the black peoples, under the colonial era, perpetuates their anthropological annihilation.[31]

The historical angle dominates this sentence.

4. Colonization is a system of anthropological pauperization, enslavement and dependence.[32]

The historical and political angles are dominant.

5. Mission and colonization, seen from an anthropological point of view, have been, in the end, agents of anthropological pauperization for the African man.[33]

Here, history and religion are most targeted.

6. Assimilation itself, which abolished our identity and our right to be different, was one of the extreme forms of anthropological pauperization.[34]

The historical angle is targeted here.

7. African poverty is an anthropological pauperization.[35]

Sociology is implicitly targeted here.

8. Men, women, families, single people, children, adults, young people, old people, the poor, the rich, the weak, the powerful, everyone in Africa is wrapped in the shroud of anthropological pauperization, which is not defined by social rank. All, whoever they are, wherever they are, are subject to its implacable tyranny.[36]

---

31. Mveng, *L'Afrique dans l'Eglise*, 206.
32. Mveng, *L'Afrique dans l'Eglise*, 207.
33. Mveng, *L'Afrique dans l'Eglise*, 207.
34. Mveng, *L'Afrique dans l'Eglise*, 208.
35. Mveng, *L'Afrique dans l'Eglise*, 210.
36. Mveng, *L'Afrique dans l'Eglise*, 210–211.

Sociology is once again targeted, as well as anthropology.

9. Africa's fragility is political; it is economic, sociological, cultural and spiritual. It is the multiple expression of its anthropological pauperization. It is the result of this ruthless system of structural pauperization.[37]

    Politics, history, sociology are targeted here.

10. The spiritual emptiness is perhaps the dramatic consequence of this pauperization.[38]

    Religion is targeted here.

11. The multiple fragility mentioned above, the anthropological pauperization at all levels and the spiritual emptiness generate misery.[39]

    The allusion to politics and religion is obvious.

12. In fact, the African context of colonization and racism is a context of anthropological annihilation. The context of postcolonial Africa is a context of anthropological pauperization. It justifies a new system of domination that is perhaps one of the most subtle and complex in human history. It presents itself as a real industry that works to perpetuate and exploit human misery considered as a real raw material.[40]

    Politics, history as well as economics are targeted.

13. The Gospel must be read by Africans, in their real context. The Gospel must answer the questions of real people in this context. To the victims of anthropological annihilation and pauperization, what does the Good News of Jesus Christ say?[41]

---

37. Mveng, *L'Afrique dans l'Eglise*, 211.
38. Mveng, *L'Afrique dans l'Eglise*, 211.
39. Mveng, *L'Afrique dans l'Eglise*, 212.
40. Mveng, *L'Afrique dans l'Eglise*, 220.
41. Mveng, *L'Afrique dans l'Eglise*, 221.

Religion is more targeted than other angles.

The main idea that emerges from this work is undoubtedly the struggle for an authentically African Christianity, but even more so that of the revalorization of African culture and the rehabilitation of the black man.

(In collaboration with B.L. Lipawing), *Théologie, Libération et Cultures Africaines. Dialogue sur l'anthropologie négro-africaine* (1996).

This is the last book Engelbert Mveng ever published. The preface was written only two days before his assassination, which makes it a testament. In this book, Engelbert Mveng addresses several topics with co-author Benjamin Lipawing. And this thematic diversity does not go without a pronounced allusion to the concept of anthropological pauperization.

Pauperization is discussed in relation to politics, history, sociology, religion, anthropology, etc.

1. In the field of intellectual and artistic creativity and in spiritual experience, man leads a struggle of self-liberation that opposes him to the image of God, creator of himself and creator of a sublimated world; there is also in this creative freedom, the refusal of determinism; whether this determinism is called oppression, politics, economy or culture, or whether it is called the mechanism of anthropological pauperization that empties man of his essence, of his dignity, of his rights, of his culture and of his capacity to create.[42]

   The religious and anthropological angles are evident here.

2. The political context, the economic context, the African cultural context appear essentially under the influence of new mechanisms of domination and oppression more rigid than those of before. The depersonalization of the African man under colonial rule was a stripping away of all that he

---

42. Mveng and Lipawing, *Théologie, Libération et cultures africaines*, 14.

was, all that he did, and the reduction to a state of indigeneity and misery that we call the state of anthropological pauperization.[43]

The political, historical and anthropological angles are the most targeted.

3. One is surprised at the abundant literature on grassroots communities (in Latin America), and the total silence that hangs over racial discrimination and the mechanisms of anthropological pauperization to which indigenous and black people are subjected.[44]

The sociological angle is the most targeted.

4. The African continent has been stripped of all its riches, not only material but also spiritual, notably its identity, its culture, its history and the multiple expressions of its faith. This is what we have called anthropological pauperization.[45]

Politics, religion as well as history are targeted here.

5. Anthropological pauperization, that is to say the state of destitution and indigence of being in post-colonial Africa, must be our first concern today. For therein lies the danger of death that hangs over Africa.[46]

Anthropology and certainly sociology are targeted.

6. In the framework of African philosophical and theological reflection, we take anthropology as our starting point, that is, man as a subject of creative thought. We also posit that, for the study of our African context, categories other than those of capitalism and Marxism must be elaborated by ourselves.

---

43. Mveng and Lipawing, *Théologie, Libération et cultures africaines*, 32.
44. Mveng and Lipawing, *Théologie, Libération et cultures africaines*, 39.
45. Mveng and Lipawing, *Théologie, Libération et cultures africaines*, 40.
46. Mveng and Lipawing, *Théologie, Libération et cultures africaines*, 65.

The Mvengian Vision of Anthropological Pauperization

> Thus, the concept of life, death or anthropological pauperization gives a much better account of our realities.[47]

> Philosophy, anthropology, theology, politics are explicitly targeted.

7. The whole point of colonization and the whole system of oppression and exploitation is to strip you of what you are, what you have and what you do. It is depersonalization, anthropological annihilation. If pauperization means to be, to become poor or to make poor, by stripping or being stripped of what one possesses, anthropological pauperization consists in stripping man of his essence, his identity, his culture, his dignity, his history, his fundamental rights, his creation, his creativity, of everything that makes up his dignity, his originality, his irreplaceable uniqueness.[48]

> History and anthropology are targeted.

8. That is why there is no African personality where there is anthropological pauperization. And what constitutes the very essence of the African personality is its heritage of being, with its culture, its traditions, its languages, its art, its conception of the world, of the man of God, and all its creative genius.[49]

> Culture, anthropology, religion are explicitly targeted.

9. When we speak of liberation, we do not give in to fashion. We denounce a reality that is staring us in the face. Philosophy, ideology, theology, spirituality appropriate in the situation of anthropological pauperization proper to our peoples today can and must only be dynamics and processes of liberation, because the African man is no longer free and is not liberated.[50]

---

47. Mveng and Lipawing, *Théologie, Libération et cultures africaines*, 91.
48. Mveng and Lipawing, *Théologie, Libération et cultures africaines*, 95.
49. Mveng and Lipawing, *Théologie, Libération et cultures africaines*, 95.
50. Mveng and Lipawing, *Théologie, Libération et cultures africaines*, 119.

The Man, His Works and His Thought

Anthropology, philosophy, theology, ideology are clearly targeted.

The main idea of this work can be summarized as follows: the fight for culture as well as the rehabilitation of man, in Africa and in the world.

At what level does the idea of anthropological pauperization arise for the first time?

Having listed the various phrases on anthropological pauperization or pauperization in general, we now need to know in which book or writing anthropological pauperization was first used.

Our research still has the seeds of a research that wants to contribute to the philosophical production in Africa. We do not claim to be exhaustive, nor do we want to be a pioneer in the study of the development of the theory of anthropological pauperization by Engelbert Mveng. Our reflection is above all philosophical. In relation to the chosen theme, we want to see if there would not be there a track of philosophical reflection on the ntù, on the African man, the African woman. Such is the goal that we pursue. That is why we thought of seeing first of, all closely, the content which gives meaning to the use of this concept.

From the three writings we have identified, it appears that it is much more in the article "Paupérsation et Développement en Afrique" that the mvengian vision of anthropological pauperization finds its final definition. How can this be so? Let us note first of all that this was published in 1992. *L'Afrique dans l'Eglise* was published in 1987, while the very last book *Théologie, Libération et Cultures Africaines* was only published in 1996.

If anthropological pauperization finds its final definition in an article, that does not mean it was the first time it was used by Engelbert Mveng. Reflecting on the first use of such a concept, we thought (we can perhaps dip our toes in the water), that it was around the years 1980–1985 or perhaps even earlier, that Engelbert Mveng first used the concept of anthropological pauperization, in his writings. In his book *L'Afrique dans l'Eglise*, he tried to gather conferences given here and there, throughout the world. Now some of them (if not all) were published in a few issues of the Bulletin de Théologie Africaine, a year or two before their publication in *L'Afrique dans l'Eglise*.

Commentary

In philosophy, each author has his own vocabulary which distinguishes him from the others. That is why, the concept of "Dasein" will make think of Heidegger, that of "Action" of Blondel; "Anthropological pauperization" makes think for sure of Engelbert Mveng.

To understand the anthropological pauperization of Mveng, it is to find oneself initially in front of a situation where it is the ntù who is in position of weakness. This positioning poses him at all costs to questioning, to philosophize.

Of all the quotations listed above, we can retain only one definition of the "anthropological pauperization": the stripping of the black man, of the ntù in all his physical, moral, cultural, religious being, etc.

His other works

The vast culture that Engelbert Mveng displayed does not merely situate him in relation to the concept of anthropological pauperization. He was a man of extremely advanced skill.

In our humble opinion and until proven otherwise, not having all of Engelbert Mveng's published and unpublished works, we have not found (apart from the writings selected above) any other writings inherent to anthropological pauperization. Does this mean that Engelbert Mveng only speaks of anthropological pauperization in the three works we have chosen? We do not pretend to assert this. But, if other works inherent to anthropological pauperization exist, we have no knowledge of them.

The Man, His Works and His Thought

It seems moreover that among these writings, the article "*Paupérisation et Développement en Afrique*" is undoubtedly one of the most eloquent, the most detailed.

Chapter Two

The Anthropological Pauperization of the Ntù

> This second chapter dissects the notion of anthropological pauperization with its five levels, trying to adapt it to the individual level. Even if Mveng approaches anthropological pauperization first at the level of state structures, we cannot forget that it is individuals who allow the State to function. A question that is raised in this chapter is whether anthropological pauperization is a process or a state of being. Applied at the individual level, this notion puts the ntù is a problematic situation that leads him to questioning. This questioning is analyzed in the five levels of anthropological pauperization. A consideration thus puts an end to this questioning.

The starting point of Negro-African thought is not being as a being. On the contrary, it is the most fundamental experience of Man, the experience of life, and of the life of the living Man. We have beforehand, not an ontology but an anthropology.[1]

---

1. Mveng, *L'Afrique dans l'Eglise*, 10.

The Anthropological Pauperization of the Ntù

AFTER HAVING SPOKEN IN the first part, about the author and his works, we are now in the second part entitled "anthropological pauperization of the ntù." There are five types of pauperization, as said above:

- Structural pauperization;
- Pseudo-philanthropic pauperization;
- Corruptive pauperization;
- Pauperization of indebtedness;
- Cultural pauperization.

The African thought is as Engelbert Mveng specifies, a thought based on anthropology, in the etymological sense of the word, that is to say the science or the study of the man. It is not a thought based on ontology:

> The doctrine of being, in any sense that we take the word being. And to speak about being, whatever the own design of every philosophy, it is always to send back to the oldest of the questions of the philosophy and consequently to repeat it: "what is"? and more radically: "what is the being for what is?"[2]

It is undoubtedly by speaking about this anthropological postulate that Engelbert Mveng ends up with the anthropological pauperization which first strips the postcolonial African State, and by ricochet, the ntù.

---

2. Nkeramihigo, *Initiation à l'acte philosophique*, 99.

The Mvengian Vision of Anthropological Pauperization

Indeed, the anthropological pauperization, like any philosophy, starts from the lived experience of man, from this social reality which, inevitably, even leads to politics.

Philosophy is of an indispensable character in our society. It must give meaning to our existence, to our life on earth. True philosophy is one which leads to politics insofar as this one is first and foremost a social reality. It is on this social reality of politics, that philosophy does not cease to ask itself questions to find solutions peculiar to men of its time (contemporaries), and perhaps even to the descendants of these.

All true philosophy, as André Gide said so well, starts from the problems that distress man. And the anthropological pauperization is part of these problems which desolate the ntù, Africa. In a bit to seek for solutions to these problems which worry the ntù so well, the recourse to a certain number of tracks is so to speak allowed. This recourse can be multiform. It is thus that one can appeal to history, to anthropology, to sociology, to politics, etc. But what is politics?

> The term "politics" comes from the Greek words polis, politeia, politica, politikè.
> -è polis: the city, the town, the country, or the meeting of the citizens who form the city;
> -è politeia: the state, the constitution, the political regime, the Republic, the citizenship (in the sense of the rights of the citizens);
> -ta politica: neuter plural of politicos, political things, civic things, everything that concerns the state, the constitution, the political regime, the Republic, sovereignty; -è politikè (technè): the political art.
> For the ancients, politica pragmateia is the study or the knowledge of the life in common of men according to the structure of this life which is the constitution of the City.[3]

The ancient man, as defined by Aristotle, appears as a being or a "civic animal." One reduces the range of the definition by

---

3. Weil quoted by Prélot, *La science politique*, 6.

The Anthropological Pauperization of the Ntù

translating zoon politikon by "social animal."[4] The animal can be social, but man, alone, is political.

As far as our subject is concerned, we think with conviction that the anthropological pauperization of the ntù constitutes an aspect not less important of this social reality that characterizes the state of being of a ntù people, the state of being of the ntù, in his material action, in his existing life.

In a word, it is a question here of the ntù as "this being or this political animal," taken in all its dimensions, social, religious, individual, etc. "The mechanisms of impoverishment, let us say it at once, do not attack only the institutions and the societies. They attack the human condition as such."[5]

It is thus above all a state of being, this anthropological pauperization, which places the man, the ntù in a context which is quite precise to him.

But is the anthropological pauperization only a state of being?

A state or a process? What is anthropological pauperization?

The words "pauperization" and "anthropology" refer respectively to poverty and to man. Put together, they simply mean the poverty of man, but of what kind of man? Of the "ntù" precisely. A being who fights to live, wants to give meaning to his existence, a being who is convinced that change is possible by dint of fighting. In short, a being who "refuses to die" or who wants to let his "cry" be heard before dying.

By "pauperization," Engelbert Mveng understands "the fact of becoming or of making poor."[6]

This said, pauperization is more a process than a state of poverty. Or better, it is a process which puts the ntù in a state which does not benefit him hardly.

---

4. Prélot, *La science politique*, 5–6.
5. Mveng, "Paupérisation et développement en Afrique," 118.
6. Mveng, "Paupérisation et développement en Afrique," 115.

The Mvengian Vision of Anthropological Pauperization

The anthropological pauperization is a whole vision that the ntù being, makes of the world. Much more than that, it is a meditation that the ntù makes of his world, of a world marked by injustice, social disengagement, oppression, lies, ignorance, etc.

Pauperization is also the state or better the process of the ntù who discovers by himself that finally it is up to him to be able to seek for his freedom. But how? How to think differently in a world which is his, but nevertheless in which he sees himself marginalized? How can he get out of this world when he is at the same time marked by it? Is he not in a problematic situation?

A concept that puts the ntù in a problematic situation.

Indeed, the pauperization puts the ntù in a problematic situation. As a concept, it is a problematic. What is it to say?

> The adjective qualifies in logic a statement that may be true, but that is not explicitly affirmed as such. The noun designates the set of problems that specify the field of a scientific research or a philosophical system, that is to say the way in which one poses the problems that determine a philosophical question.[7]

In our opinion, if it is necessary to give a sense to this problematic in which the ntù is found, we would gladly opt for the very last definition: "the way in which one poses the problems that determine a philosophical question."

This way of seeing, Engelbert Mveng perceived it not without relevance. And a certain onomasiology (study of the expression of ideas) can lead us to say, to pastich a definition, that "the way in which Engelbert Mveng perceives the anthropological pauperization of the ntù, poses the problems that determines a philosophical question." This philosophical question can be summarized as follows: "Am I or am I not master of my destiny?" Or "How can I (me ntù) change my fate in a tormented Africa?"

---

7. Durozoi and Roussel, *Dictionnaire de philosophie*, 268.

The Anthropological Pauperization of the Ntù

Therefore, the questions raised here are indeed problematic because they are philosophical or problematized because they determine a philosophical question: that of fate and desired destiny of the ntù.

> I am not an economist. I am only a man of the Third World, a son of African peasants, crushed by the crisis, and who, joining my voice to that of my people, proclaim to the world that we refuse to die. We refuse to die under the weight of this crisis that makes the prosperity of some and the misery of others. We want to know why the world today seems irrevocably divided into two universes: the universe of development, wealth, prosperity, domination and power, and the universe of underdevelopment, misery, poverty, dependence, dominated and powerless people. We ask ourselves why this one is the universe of others, and why this one is our universe.[8]

In this sentence, Engelbert Mveng raises not without relevance the problem of poverty, and thus of the pauperization, which is the universe of the ntù. It is a real cry of heart which cannot leave indifferent (unless they are inhuman) those who live in the other universe.

The problem here posed by Engelbert Mveng, is not to make pass the ntù from the universe of pauperization, poverty, to the universe of wealth. It is thus not a question of a transfer of the universes, but rather of change of the conditions of life, to be, without obligatorily changing universe. These two universes were not created in this way. But men by their malice and their selfishness, called this universe of the "rich countries" and that one universe of the "poor countries," "underdeveloped," or universe of the "developing countries."

To borrow an image, the ntù looks like a prisoner who does not know the reason of his imprisonment and does not know why he is there. Why only the ntù and not another one? Why only "me" and not another person? This is the fundamental question, the question that every ntù being asks himself.

---

8. Mveng, "Paupérisation et développement en Afrique," 111.

The Mvengian Vision of Anthropological Pauperization

In a word, the problematic posed by the mvengian vision of the anthropological pauperization, brings the ntù to a questioning of the status quo. A status quo that wants to make him believe that, by his essence, he is dominable, subjected to a master, and therefore inferior. That is to say a dominating ideology.

To do this, we notice not without satisfaction that Mveng elaborated that in system,—and not just any system—, an increasingly elaborated that has, in its bosom, all the dimensions of the life of the ntù. The mastery of all these dimensions can lead the ntù to change his fate in a desired destiny. This is not impossible.

This is undoubtedly what makes Engelbert Mveng's originality, his strength, to have perceived with clarity and relevance, the stakes of this anthropological pauperization.

Indeed, such as elaborated, anthropological pauperization effectively puts the ntù in a situation undoubtedly of the most problematic. Not only does it not allow the ntù to live freely, but it leads him to phenomenal asphyxia. As for the noumenal asphyxia that it also tries to undertake—without fortunately succeeding—, anthropological pauperization, seeing itself at the end of its strength, wants finally to strangle the ntù, to eliminate him once for all. But, impregnated of this "vital force" which characterizes him, the ntù refuses to die under the weight of the burden. He reflects or better thinks his situation in the hope that one day, he will be finally depauperized, in order to enjoy a better tomorrow.

But, if pauperization clearly reveals a problem, it emerges that behind this same problem, lies indeed an existential crisis. Through anthropological pauperization, it is the life of the ntù that is threatened. It is indeed, a real threat of death to which the ntù says: "no, I refuse to die." Such is the protest of "all those who do not want to die."[9]

In other words, anthropological pauperization is the pronounced refusal of an Africa that is still in a bad way. In short, the refusal of an "Africaninism."[10] It is therefore the refusal of a way of

---

9. Mveng and Lipawing, *Théologie, Libération et cultures africaines*, 7. See also Kanza, *Non. Je ne mourrai pas, je vivrai*.

10. By this term, we mean the external and internal turmoil that Africa has

doing things, overwhelming, towards the choice of a better life, of a black Africa well on its way, that is to say of an "Africanitude."[11]

Also, it should be emphasized that, in Mveng, anthropological pauperization is different from anthropological annihilation.

> When it comes to slavery and colonization, we are talking about anthropological annihilation. It is not genocide, because the Negro, because of his physical strength and his aptitude for manual labor, was a sought-after and valuable commodity. Anthropological annihilation strips him of his human instruments, to reduce him to the state of a beast of burden, to instrumentalize him, to commodify him. After independence, it is poverty that now creates a new system of dependence. This system, in order to base its legitimacy, calls for international solidarity, assistance, cooperation, in short, a whole philanthropic apparatus that serves as a cover for the apparatus of domination.[12]

The five levels of anthropological pauperization

As mentioned above, there are five levels of anthropological pauperization.

a) Structural pauperization of the ntù:

> There is the level of the essence of the structure, of the institutions of the State. This level is mainly due to the historical circumstances of the advent to independence.

experienced and continues to experience in other forms. Africaninism (not Africanism) is the Africa denied (hence the first "ni") by slavery, colonization, etc. It is also Africa which denies (this is where the second "ni" comes in) and re-denies itself (internal wars, conflicts of all kinds between Africans leading to compromises and not to agreements, refusal of development, betrayal of Africa, etc.).

11. By this other term, which is in fact only the reverse of the one that precedes it (Africaninism), we give an opposite definition.

12. Mveng, "Paupérisation et développement en Afrique," 118.

The Mvengian Vision of Anthropological Pauperization

It is largely a legacy of colonization. Pauperization is at this level structural.[13]

In structural pauperization, Engelbert Mveng insists much more on the post-colonial African State. We will lean more on the subject ntù.

In his environment, the ntù is questioned. The level of "the essence," of "the structure," says Engelbert Mveng, and of the institutions of State, question his existence, his rights to live free and with dignity.

For Engelbert Mveng, structural anthropological pauperization is mainly due to the historical circumstances of the advent of independence. This level is, he adds, "a legacy of colonization." Here, the ntù is thus in a situation which does not advantage him. He sees himself called into question first by colonization, then by the institutions of the State, reflection of the colonial machine. His problematic and bipolar situation then appears. Hence the following diagram:

Figure01

1) White   **Ntù**

(The other)

2) Ntù   **Another Ntù**

If the relationship of the other to the ntù can be the object of excuses (we do not want to minimize here the colonization of the ntù, but what we insist on is the fact that the ntù found himself reified by the other, the White), what about the ntù who would let himself be reified by another ntù, by his brother of skin, his brother of blood? Would this one receive less excuses than this other (White)? If so, why?

First of all, it is necessary to point out that the ntù who diminishes his blood or skin brother, is not different from the one he mistreats. Both are in a situation where they appear as hostages of

---

13. Mveng, "Paupérisation et développement en Afrique," 115.

The Anthropological Pauperization of the Ntù

a system that, to survive, needs "mercenaries" for the control of the established order. The ntù who mistreats his brother ntù is not free because he works for a master. Because the conditions in which he lives are unfortunate he is "forced" to accept to lead a kind of "Vie et demie."[14] He thus leads a more or less "appeased" life.

On the other hand, the ntù "pauperized" by his brother of blood, undergoes (and it is there where he differs from his brother of blood) a kind of pauperization with double facet.

However, if the Other (White) appears as the man of whom it is necessary to "get rid of" (this does not mean to kill but rather to tumble the way of acting, of doing), the bought ntù (the man with "a life and a half "), appears as the one who must also be freed from the oppressor. That is to say that the question posed at the beginning to know if he would receive less excuses than the Other (White), is thus not posed any more with the same fervor, it must be nuanced.

Indeed, Engelbert Mveng perceived the problem with relevance. Structural pauperization is very dangerous, because it did not let the ntù breathe only one moment of his life. It is all the more dangerous because it attacks the ntù in his schemes of thought, in his intimate life and thus in his very quintessence. Through structural pauperization , the ntù is reached in his "spinal cord." It is an "abysmal" attack which leaves enormous damage in its wake. Let us think first of all of the socio-structural destructions (the acute conscience that the ntù had before the colonization, where did it go?)

Indeed, nowadays, many Africans are unaware of what Africa was like before the arrival of the white man. The consequences have been enormous, to the extent that knowing one's family tree today has become almost impossible. When asked about their family tree, children can barely remember their great grandparents. We may be exaggerating, but the point remains that much of this is true.

Here, we are at the level of the individual or individuals. At the level of state institutions, we are witnessing a similar equation.

---

14. Life and a half. See Sony Labou Tansi, La vie et demie (1979).

African states have inherited colonization. Our States are from the beginning, the reflection of the Western States. What were our countries then, long before? We ignore it or we pretend to ignore it. However, we know that long before the arrival of the Westerners, democracy existed in Africa. One of its forms in the past was the palaver.

"The palaver, says Engelbert Mveng, was presented as the most popular model of democracy."[15] Its use "extended from the family to the state. In the formerly "anarchic" societies (Congo, Gabon, Equatorial Guinea and South Cameroon), as well as in the great empires of West Africa, the basins of Congo and Zambezi." [16]

Still according to Mveng, the African palaver was based on two principles. The first was "the right to speak to all" (to express the sovereignty of the people); and the second principle was "the search for consensus" (a democracy rather conciliatory than competitive).

All these riches were unfortunately annihilated, pauperized, with the arrival of colonization. This is Eurocentrism, Western imperialism, which only saw the African as a barbarian, an irrational man.

This example of the palaver simply shows how abysmal structural pauperization has been by plunging the ntù into an unforgettable oblivion because it is too deep, or by making the ntù a truly alienated being.

In other words, structural pauperization through colonization, is all at once, all these demolished kingdoms, these empires, destroyed or weakened dynasties.

Engelbert Mveng also points out that, "the colonial period, in Africa, is a gaping hiatus in the history of our continent. "[17]

---

15. Mveng and Lipawing, *Théologie, libération et cultures africaines*, 221.
16. Mveng and Lipawing, *Théologie, libération et cultures africaines*, 221.
17. Mveng and Lipawing, *Théologie, libération et cultures africaines*, 225.

b) Pseudo-philanthropic pauperization of the ntù:

Then there is the level of assistance. It is the level of the lack of compassion. In fact, says Father Mveng, the mechanisms of pauperization tend to maintain the state of dependence and domination under the mask of the help and the assistance. The pauperization at this level is pseudo-philanthropic.[18]

With regard to pseudo-philanthropic pauperization, the ntù is in a position such as he is the object of recovery, of servant used of the "Other." He is not the beneficiary, but the great loser. Thus, what should be his by right is taken away from him in fact. He is stripped, weakened, made passive, unfit for action and therefore dependent on everything, dominated "under the mask of help and assistance." In addition to this, he is a prisoner of the initiatives of the Other, a victim of not daring to think for himself.

This state is none other than the deceptive, ruinous, shameful, alarming, masked situation in which the ntù is. A situation that pushes all the more to make us think. Because, the victim looks like a butterfly whose wings have been removed, and that we send back in the air as if to ask it to fly.

The possibility of action and re-action of the ntù is as if limited, measured. In other words, he resembles a goat tied to a rope, and which can only graze according to the length of the rope. It is here that the mask of the assistance appears. The goat is assisted by the one who has placed it near the tree as if to signify that it is there to serve it; which is unfortunately false. By taking this image, we do not say that the ntù is a goat, but that his possibilities to move freely in dignity are limited.

Today, there are complaints that human rights are not respected in some parts of the world, especially in Africa. However, it is noted with indignation that the so-called human rights are not respected at the state or institutional level. But when it directly threatens the ntù in his corporality, it is said that human rights are scorned. And when institutions are targeted, we speak of S.A.P.

---

18. Mveng, "Paupérisation et développement en Afrique, " 115–116.

(Structural Adjustment Program) whose operating rules unfortunately did not allow African countries to function freely. This is also pseudo-philanthropic pauperization: tying a rope around someone's neck and telling him that he is free, that he can run as he likes, as long as the rope is not taken away.

Another characteristic of this same pseudo-philanthropic pauperization is the maintenance of the status quo. Maintaining the status quo is synonymous with not allowing the ntù, the African States to live the way they want, but rather asking permission when it comes to carrying out such an undertaking likely to allow them to "take off" economically, politically, scientifically, etc.

In a word, it is a system that does not want the ntù to escape it in his way of doing things, a system that does not want that the ntù to surpass it economically, politically, and even scientifically. In other words, not to allow him to develop. This is unfortunately accepted by some impolitical politicians who prostitute themselves for money, happiness, wealth, honors and respect purchased that make them corrupt ntù.

c) Corruptive pauperization of the ntù:

> Then comes in the third place, the level of corruption. It is actually a system of looting entire peoples and countries through the mediation of alleged leaders or elites loaded with golden chains. We can call this form: corrupt pauperization.[19]

Corruptive pauperization puts the ntù in a position of weakness; it undergoes a "dictatorship" without limits with the complicity of "pretended chiefs or elites in charge of golden chains" who are unfortunately bought, corrupted ntù. The ntù, ntù among all the other weakened, pauperized ntù of the mass, is forced to beg for life because there are no other outcomes for him than this one.

Corruptive pauperization reaches its peak with the looting orchestrated by people who really don't like Africa, and who are

---

19. Mveng, "Paupérisation et développement en Afrique, " 116.

The Anthropological Pauperization of the Ntù

able of giving their heads to cut, so that Africa is always on the wrong track.

The bad thing about this pauperization is that the certain participation of the sons of Africa allows us to say with Axelle Kabou, that indeed Africa refuses development.[20] But perhaps these words should be nuanced in order to avoid certain misinterpretations. Africa refuses development, according to the behavior of some of its leaders, not all of them of course. The situation is becoming more and more problematic because those who display such behavior are indeed those who have power and decide.

At the same time, voices are being raised here and there to refuse to maintain the status quo, and demand change. Unfortunately, these voices do not have power, they do not have money, which makes the power of others.

What, on the one hand, slows down is undoubtedly this too small number of leaders able to raise their voices, to drain entire peoples in order to bring about the long-awaited change.

On the other hand, there is a kind of lack of social courage among peoples to, like one voice, shout this change in unison. It is therefore a kind of sociological pusillanimity that keeps the people in the status quo. But perhaps this is due to the non-education suffered by this people, which non-education is probably a reflection of a well-thought-out system (itself corrupt), whose mechanisms to shake it would have to be carefully studied. This is not at all easy, because this same system tries day by day to stay in time.

d) Pauperization of the indebtedness of the ntù:

> The most overwhelming pauperization is undoubtedly that of Debt. It is a system of enslavement of entire peoples and countries, condemned to work in perpetuity, for an unknown master. Supposedly, to repay usurious debts, that the people have not contracted.[21]

---

20. Kabou, *Et si l'Afrique refusait le développement?*
21. Mveng, "Paupérisation et développement en Afrique," 116.

Among all these pauperizations, the most oppressive, says Engelbert Mveng, is that of the indebtedness, because it maintains the ntù in a perpetual situation of slavery, for a seemingly unkown master.

But rather let's try to understand why Engelbert Mveng describes this pauperization of indebtedness, of "the most overwhelming."

It seems to us that, this is all the more true for the simple reason that in our world, money is considered to be absolute master, for whoever wants to get rich, wants to live with dignity. Or, any society that wants to maintain itself must first have money.

Experience has proven it, when some parts of sub-Saharan Africa are said to be "rich" (which is probably true), it is only because they have a rich subsoil. But since they do not have what allows them to transform these raw materials into consumer products, it is therefore difficult to talk about this wealth, which is only passive. This passive wealth that Africans claim with so much pride carries a real danger, if it does not allow them to make it active, i.e. productive. Otherwise, it will make Africans onlookers in need of occupation spending their time contemplating it all day long. This happens in the streets.

e) Cultural pauperization of ntù:

> The fifth level is that of cultural pauperization. Almost all of the Black African States have kept intact the colonial legacy of cultural pauperization . . . The negro-African States have gained independence amid the ruins of their society in disarray.[22]

The last pauperization says Mveng, is the cultural pauperization. The ntù looks like a being who ignores his history, his culture.

Engelbert Mveng notes with indignation that "Almost all of the Black African States have kept intact the colonial legacy of cultural pauperization."

22. Mveng, "Paupérisation et développement en Afrique," 116.

The Anthropological Pauperization of the Ntù

This cultural pauperization, just like the previous ones, does not benefit the ntù, and makes him more and more alienated, dependent on the assistance and the mask of the compassion of the other.

Indeed, the ntù to learn about the affairs of his country, largely uses a language that is not African. Let us think of all our Constitutions and laws written mostly in foreign languages. For Engelbert Mveng, these languages are "impenetrable for 80% of the population." And when it comes to schooling, textbooks reach us, written in these same foreign languages. As long as the Agreements or cultural Conventions are not revised so that the ntù finds his advantage, this cultural pauperization of which we are all victims, thinks Mveng, will continue to make victims, and the future of things will escape us.

What is deplorable, it is that these Agreements or cultural Conventions perpetuate cultural pauperization "with millions tons of textbooks, and legions of advisers and technical assistants with often indiscreet zeal, betraying cultural oppression under the mask of assistance.[23]

The consequences of this cultural pauperization, according to Engelbert Mveng, are enormous. There are for example: the loss of the heritage of traditional religions, spiritual pauperization with the arrival of imported religions, the moral and spiritual vacuum seriously exploited by secret societies and sects, etc.

As mentioned above, if there anthropological pauperization, it is mainly that of the ntù. What did Engelbert Mveng mean? What was he looking for when talking about anthropological pauperization?

A consideration

> It is impossible for a man to seek neither what he knows nor what he does not know. Neither on the one hand what he knows, he would seek it, because he knows it,

---

23. Mveng, "Paupéristion et développement en Afrique, " 116.

and in such a case he does not need to seek it; nor on the other hand what he does not know, because he does not know what he will have to look for.[24]

The primary concern that would have led Engelbert Mveng to reflect on the situation of the ntù, is probably that this ntù was not considered part of the history. The Negro as he will call him was therefore on the periphery of human history.

It was thus necessary to revalue him and make him aware of the urgency for him, to take his desired destiny into his own hands. Treated like a subman, he could not fail to ask himself these questions linked to existential ethics and personal ethics. "Am I not like the others?" or "Should I live or should I not live?" or "My life, on whom does it depend?"

The situation of the ntù in anthropological pauperization is, a problematic that must at all costs question any African philosopher asking himself questions related to his environment, his existence and therefore consequently to his future.

It is therefore clear that the ntù in the case of structural pauperization (as well as the other four types of pauperization) is initially confronted with an existential problem in his relationship with others than in his relationship with himself and his society.

---

24. Socrates quoted by Gusdorf, *Pourquoi des philosophes?*, 196.

CHAPTER THREE

Critique and Contribution of Anthropological Pauperization of the Ntù in African Philosophy

> In this third chapter, a criticism of the notion of anthropological pauperization is made. At the same time, it is a question of emphasizing the contribution of this same notion to African philosophy. Concretly, it is a question of pointing out the limits of this concept, its contribution to the way of philosophizing in Africa, not to mention the issues raised as well as the challenges facing the ntù.

Limits

AS FAR AS PHILOSOPHICAL, scientific or theological production is concerned, each thinker always starts from a problem that he raises from certain interrogations. But history has shown us at the same time that absolute thoughts do not exist, that there is no thinker who can stand as the sole possessor of the truth. So much so that in the thought of an author, whoever he is and despite the relevance of his thought, there are always limits in his way of conceiving the reality of things. In other words, every philosophical, theological, scientific, historical, etc. work is never a perfect work; it has parts in it that deserve to be enlightened, to be nuanced. For if it were not so, we would all stop philosophizing to the extent that we would have already reached the whole truth and nothing but the truth.

This is also noticed in the path made by an author. There are certain imperfections that he discovers for himself, and others, on the other hand, that some thinkers or critics make him discover.

It is undoubtedly the same, for the one for whom we study the theory: Engelbert Mveng.

Indeed, Engelbert Mveng says in his writings (Mveng 1985: 10) that it is the vital force—repeating Placide Tempels— that constitutes the starting point of Negro- African philosophy.

Is such a vision, which is erected into an interpretation of life and an exaltation of the vital force, sufficient -when we know that it takes up African cultural traditions previously denied and makes the black person a human being who also exists, in the same way as the other human beings on earth- to make it correspond to the beginning of the philosophy or the history of the Negro- African philosophy?

In addition, talking about African philosophy starting with the work of Placide Tempels seems somewhat exaggerated. We therefore think that Engelbert Mveng is historically mistaken on this point. Why? Simply because, if we admit with Professor Théopile Obenga that "the history of African philosophy obviously follows the framework of the general history of the African continent as a whole and, chronologically,"[1] it seems to us therefore regrettable that Professor Engelbert Mveng entitled several years before his thesis *Les sources grecques de l'histoire négro-africaine, depuis Homère jusqu'à Strabon*, and at the same time, he begins this same philosophy with Tempels' work. Didn't Greek thinkers once went to Egypt to study mathematics, geometry, philosophy, etc.?

If really, the history of philosophy follows the framework of the general history of Africa, why then to have started this philosophy with Tempels' work as if it were with the latter that philosophy

---

1. Obenga, *La philosophie africaine de la période pharaonique*, 13.

Critique and Contribution

was born in Africa? Mveng, didn't he know that African philosophy existed long before the arrival of these missionaries on African soil?

According to Obenga, in his book: *La philosophie africaine de la période pharaonique: 2780–330 avant notre ère,*[2] there are five (5) periods that allow us to read this history of the Negro-African philosophy. First, there is the:

> Egyptian philosophy, pharaonic, since the Old Kingdom (2780–3260 BC), with the texts of the Pyramids, the Inscription of Shabaka, the Maxims or Teachings of Kagemni and Prahholep"; then the "philosophers and thinkers of Alexandria, Cyrene, Carthage and Hippo," followed by "Maghreb philosophy," then the medieval philosophical schools of Timbuktu (university of Sankarè), Gao, Djené, centers of Negro-Muslim culture at the time of the great Sudanese empires (Ghana, Mali, Gou, Songhoy). " And finally, comes "modern and contemporary African philosophy."[3]

The history of African philosophy is, in one way or another, part of the Africa's history. If there are reasons to relate Negro-African history to that of African philosophy, it is probably because it is the same and only continent, Africa. Moreover, between these two types of history, bridging is possible, as Théophile Obenga says.

In the preface to the same book by Théophile Obenga, the Congolese philosopher (from Kinshasa) Tshiamalenga Ntumba expresses himself in these terms:

> The African philosophy of the pharaonic period, such is the title of an essential work, of exceptional scientific value written by a learned historian, Egyptologist and philosopher: Professor Théophile Obenga. (. . .) Professor Théophile Obenga offers us, finally, an authentic history of African philosophy really starting from the beginning . . . from the beginning attested by the oldest

---

2. *African philosophy: The Pharaonic Period: 2780–330 BC.*
3. Obenga, *La philosophie africaine de la période pharaonique*, 13–15.

philosophical writings, those of Pharaonic Egypt of the Ancient Empire.[4]

It is certainly true that *L'Afrique dans l'Eglise* by Engelbert Mveng was published five years (1985) before *La philosophie africaine de la période pharaonique* by Théophile Obenga (1990), but it seems that Mveng forgot that African philosophy predates Tempels' work.

Starting the history of African philosophy with Tempels' book (*La philosophie bantoue*) is therefore not reasonable.

We do not confront the historical problematic of an African philosophy (a specific question is raised) and the subsequent work of the historian who goes back in time and finds antecedents. To ignore this is also to forget that we are in front of a professional historian (Mveng) who gives his point of view on a precise philosophical question.

History now knows where to start this African philosophy. However, the provocative and historical work by Placide Tempels should not be minimized. The latter seems to have lit the fire, which Obenga (including all critical philosophers or admirers of Tempels) has extinguished. We can criticize Tempels today, but we cannot blame him for the fact that he dared to "start" the debate officially.

What could be the limits of anthropological pauperization?

With his theory of the anthropological pauperization, Engelbert Mveng begins and interprets the experience of the ntù, the black man. He also tries using African traditions, to value black culture, which has been long denied. In other words, Mveng makes the defense of the black person. The approach under which he makes this defense, does not seem sterile, since Mveng, through African traditions and culture, finally achieves satisfactory results. He approaches Africa's problems with such relevance, that he carries his analysis in depth.

But, if the aim (emancipation and liberation of the ntù) of such an approach is about to be achieved, the fact remains that the

---

4. Tshiamalenga in Obenga, *La philosophie africaine de la période pharaonique*, 8.

Critique and Contribution

object pursued (the return to the African cultural and traditional values) is even less so. Engelbert Mveng does not allow the ntù to lead with effectiveness the fight for liberation. By this, it can be admitted that one of the flaws of this theory is that it criticizes the functioning of the post-colonial African State, without showing the ntù the methods or means to fight against this kind of death proposed to him. Pauperization certainly appears here as a fight, but one of the characters only receives blows, without trying to defend himself properly.

In other words, Mveng does not give us effective means to overcome this pauperization, or to avoid the advance of this existential crisis that is anthropological pauperization.

The contribution of anthropological pauperization to philosophical reflection

Even if limits appear in Mvengian thought, it must always be recognized that this same thought gives philosophical research material to think about.

First of all, it must be recognized that the fight led by Mveng is a legitimate fight that has a relevant thought and cannot be the object of any intellectual nor philosophical entertainment. Mveng's thought, through his theory of anthropological pauperization, is an actualized thought that is rooted in the present and allows us to look to the past and the future. To take an image, the mvengian vision of anthropological pauperization resembles three vertically drawn lines. The first (the one on the right) being the future, the second (the one in the middle) the line of the present and the third (the one on the left), the line of the past. And Mveng himself is placed in the middle, so that he can project his gaze to the left (the past), as well as to the right (the future), or stop where he is placed, that is, the present.

In other words, the theory of anthropological pauperization has a real impact on political power in Africa, on philosophical thought, and on African societies.

It has a political impact because it is first and foremost a questioning of the way post-colonial African States work. The questions it raises, if taken seriously, can lead our leaders to think and implement an effective African policy, on the sole condition that it benefits our states and peoples.

Its impact on philosophical thought is justified insofar as philosophy encompasses the human experience, whatever it may be. In this sense, pauperization is a "place" where Africans can concretely reflect on their problems. The results obtained will undoubtedly have an impact on the problems facing African societies.

The philosophy of pauperization is a kind of hermeneutics of African societies, criticism of these same societies and a self- criticism at the same time.

Engelbert Mveng has, through his writings, his thought, the actuality and the relevance of this one, almost indelibly imprinted his signature in the sphere of the great thinkers of this African land. The number of his disciples, it is only a projection, will increase as long as his thought will continue to have an impact on our continent.

In the same perspective, it is necessary to recognize that Mveng opted for the construction of an authentic African thought.

About forty years ago, Professor Pierre Meinrad Hebga pleaded for African forms of thought through his famous article, "Eloge de l'ethnophilosophie" (1982).[5] In this article, in fact, Hebga "indicates the weaknesses of the criticism, in total "disappointing" and outrageously simplistic that Towa, Elungu, Hountondji and related exert against what they call, peremptorily, 'ethnophilosophy.'"[6] According to the philosopher Ngoma Binda, "Hebga is right to denounce this attitude and to plead for the forms of thought specific to Africa."[7]

It is undoubtedly to these "forms of thought specific to Africa," that the Mvengian vision of anthropological pauperization has contributed. To do this, it has a stake.

5. Hebga, "Eloge de l'ethnophilosophie", 20–41.
6. Ngoma Binda, *La philosophie africaine contemporaine*, 180.
7. Ngoma Binda, *La philosophie africaine contemporaine*, 181.

Critique and Contribution

The stakes of the problem

Anthropological pauperization reveals a major issue. It seems that what must be emphasized is the fact that Mveng dared to innovate, if not to direct political or even philosophical reflection, or even the debate on Black African thought, towards a different kind of African philosophizing.

Indeed, for too long we have been taught to philosophize about metaphysics, being as being, about the phenomenon and about the noumenon, to the extent that we ourselves were incapable of philosophizing about our own reality.

The problem raised by Mveng is a question of life and death for the ntù, for all the Africans and the whole of Africa. It challenges every African and all Africa worthy of the name.

Mveng has made it his task to reflect less on Africa's underdevelopment, but even more on poverty. For he says, " . . . I will not talk about DEVELOPMENT. It is their universe (rich countries) they talk too much about it, for themselves, not for us. I won't even talk about underdevelopment, which is the other side of their coin. I will only talk about our universe, which is the universe of poverty."[8]

One of the angles—among several—under which he approaches this poverty, is that of politics, through the image of the post-colonial African State. And it is there this issue probably appears, because here opens this "way of effectiveness of philosophy and to which the philosopher must turn", which is, insists Ngoma Binda, "the political path", way that Mveng used, very explicitly.

We do not want here to reduce philosophy to politics, even less to current affairs. We are interested in politics because it is part of human experience. At the same time, we notice that Mveng started from there to talk about anthropological pauperization. This means that if philosophy has as its object the entirety of human experience, politics cannot be spared.

For Ngoma Binda, in fact, "Philosophy in Africa must, therefore, largely be articulated on the criticism of Africa's dictatorial

---

8. Mveng, "Paupérisation et développement en Afrique, " 111.

regimes, capitalist as well as socialist, in order to liberate the suffering, starving, illiterate masses, freedomless masses. This liberation of the masses is a condition of efficiency of philosophy."[9]

Challenge of anthropological pauperization, as highlighted above, is therefore high. It gives not only food for thought to politicians (including impolitical politicians), but also to philosophers, anthropologists, historians, sociologists, etc.

The analysis made by Mveng, showed that pauperization was approached from several angles: political, anthropological, sociological, historical, philosophical, theological, etc. At the same time, this analysis stimulates us to meet a certain number of challenges.

The challenges of anthropological pauperization: a cultural liberation

> The fight we are leading for culture is a fight for the dignity and integrity of man, in Africa and in the world . . . Deprived of our cultural roots, we are all hostages in the jails of Anti-Culture.[10]

Anthropological pauperization undoubtedly involves several challenges. But these can be summarized in one: the cultural liberation of the ntù, which differentiates it from others. "Our revolution must first be a cultural revolution, a revolution in the conception of man,"[11] insists Engelbert Mveng.

Culture for Mveng is a whole vision that encompasses all the vital dimensions of man, his experience, his concrete actions. It is a culture that is specific to Black-African man, the ntù. Is it not that "what distinguishes peoples, is the cultural"?[12]

Indeed, after giving the different contours and detours of this anthropological pauperization, Engelbert Mveng offers us

---

9. Ngoma Binda, *La philosophie africaine contemporaine*, 181.
10. Mveng and Lipawing, *Théologie, libération et cultures africaines*, 7.
11. Mveng and Lipawing, *Théologie, libération et cultures africaines*, 7.
12. Bibaki, *Sango Ya Kimwenza*, 10.

Critique and Contribution

a cultural liberation, to allow the ntù and Africa, to solve their problems.

What does cultural liberation mean for the poor who are hungry and who expect an immediate solution to their hunger? What does cultural liberation mean for all these Africans who survive, strangled by misery, oppression and dictatorship ? In other words, does cultural liberation advocated by Engelbert Mveng have a meaning and an impact in finding solutions to all refugees, mothers, children, victims of wars and ethnic conflicts?

If cultural liberation cannot provide a material solution to the ntù, it still allows him to keep his identity.

> Only a cultural revolution can now bring about notable qualitative changes . . . Africa can only be saved by the integral patriotism of its sons.[13]

13. Anta Diop, *Antériorité des civilisations nègres*, 278.

CHAPTER FOUR

Mveng and His Heritage[1]

> This chapter came from a conference given more than two decades ago. This is a reflection made two years after Mveng's assassination. This reflection starts from this well-known African saying that compares the desappearence of an old/woman to a library that is consumed. Mveng's death is comparable to a burning library. We point out that Mveng was a character for whom there was or no sympathy. Then, his strong personality honored the expression of a free thought certainly, but above all fertile by its manifestations. A citizen of the world, Mveng placed Africa at the center of his reflections. This son of the terroir, to this day, continues to inspire other young Africans because of his fertile thought. This is where the legacy he has bequeathed to future generations is understood. A legacy marked by the rooting, conversion of civilizations, etc.

---

1. H.-H. Kibangou. This is an extract of an unpublished conference by the author of this book, between 1997 and 1998, during the first Mveng days at the Faculty of Philosophy St. P. Canisius of Kimwenza, in Kinshasa (DR Congo).

Mveng and His Heritage

Is it necessary to introduce?

It is important to recall here that Engelbert Mveng was this intellectual, this priest and this African Jesuit who, thanks to the intelligence given to him by God, tried as much as possible, to restore to Africa and this without complacency or false modesty—its true place. This made him an authentic African, son of the soil, concerned with reflecting and finding solutions to the problems that plague our continent.

A consideration

A famous maxim makes Africans admit that when " an old man dies, it is a library that burns " (Amadou Hampâte Bâ 1960). According to the explanation given by Hampâte Bâ, the old man is the one who knows. In other words, this qualifier does not necessarily refer to age. Rather, it refers to knowledge.[2] In addition, given that the old men who give initiation, have lived a long time and have experienced many things in their lives, it can be considered that these old men people advanced in age initiate the youngest in life. In this sense, Mveng was this old man, who knew and could initiate the youngest through his knowledge. Was that the reason to kill him? We say no. But now, human wickedness snatched him from us with force and suddenly. Why such a violent death?

Mveng was not only this "old man," he was also this library that not only burned, but still burns. Why burn a library instead of waiting for it to burn on its own ? We will never say it enough, Mveng is this library which continues to burn in us.

Engelbert Mveng did not die without heirs. Yes, we Africans, we his brothers, his sisters, we African Jesuits are indeed the heirs of Mveng's work. Under no circumstances do we want to appropriate his merit, but we want to affirm his particularity in the midst of the other particularities that we are.

---

2. https://esmaparis1.com/2018/02/14/en-afrique-quand-un-vieillard-meurt-cest-une-bibliotheque-qui-brule/amp/

Nor is it a question of overwhelming ourselves with what Mveng left. Certainly, Mveng's work is undoubtedly his work, but this work must not remain a dead letter. This work should find fertile land where it can grow without being worried. It is up to us to take Mveng's work so that it grows among us.

Two ways to follow

It would be insane, thus, to remain indifferent to the originality of such a character, because the feeling that one can feel towards people of Mveng's caliber is bipolar: either one feels sympathy for him, or one does not feel sympathy at all. Disputes have no place here.

Our presentation is divided into two parts: the first part is entitled "L'honneur de penser librement" (The honor of thinking freely) and the second part "Notre part d'héritage" (Our share of heritage).

The honor of thinking freely

The honor of thinking was undoubtedly one of Engelbert Mveng 's concerns. His numerous publications and his commitment to the intellectual apostolate are rather a convincing example.

Mveng granted a very important place to freedom. In his vision, no one was excluded. Hence his determination not to be fooled by those who thought that the Black person did not have the right to freedom. In the name of this freedom, he denounced the violation of the association pact by a few individuals.

Who can deprive man of his freedom to live, to pray, to think, in short to remain fully himself? No one except God. Having thus understood this, Mveng could not admit that freedom of expression was taken away from him. And this was felt in Mveng's experience. This freedom of expression took various forms: in his speech, in his writings, and in art. He could then implement this intelligence that God gave him, convinced that the absence of thought, and therefore the absence of freedom, "is more to be feared than the most characterized wickedness, stupidity or ignorance."[3]

Thinking his society and his world in a tormented Africa

During his life, Mveng reflected on his situation as an African, as a religious in an Africa victim of intermittent turmoil. His vision of the world, including Africa, matured in this reflection.

The mvengian vision of the world is a vision that believes in the liberation of our world. To free the suffering majority in the face of an overwhelming minority. Such is the paradox of our world. The fewest because they have money, power, mistreat the most numerous. This situation, insists the historian, is that of a sick world. Therefore he does not prevent himself from recognizing in the preface to his posthumous book that:

> Today's world is very sick. Humanity, mostly starved, oppressed, reduced to misery, is nothing more than a defenseless rag, struggling with the hordes of Death, unleashed by the insatiable monsters that hold Power and Wealth and are almost all from the countries of the North. The technological civilization of this end of the twentieth century, generator of this enormous industry of terror, misery and death, is therefore only an anti-culture, a formidable perversion of man's relations, with nature, with God.[4]

As can be seen, between Mveng and Africa, a frank, engaging and engaged dialogue had been established. He could not admit that his black brothers and sisters, suffer continuously. Reflecting in this way, he came to the conclusion that God had nothing to do with our misfortune; God has not cursed Africa. It is man and his wickedness that cause so much misfortunes to our continent. In short, Africa is also sick; but it is not condemned to be so.

---

3. Eboussi, *Terroirs*, 3.
4. Mveng and Lipawing, *Théologie, libération et cultures africaines*, 5.

> We are one of those who do not believe that Africa is condemned. Sick indeed, Africa is sick in the middle of an equally sick world (...)
> Africa is indeed sick, stuck between the relentless claws of these sinful structures that imprison the world in which we live, under the law of the fool's market where the rich will always be rich and the poor ever poorer.[5]

In the face of such a struggle, should we remain silent? No. On the contrary, we must fight so that Africa is not condemned to suffer. The survival of the continent is at stake, and therefore our survival. Hence the refusal to die.

> We refuse to die under the weight of this crisis that makes the prosperity of some and the misery of others. We want to know why the world today seems irrevocably divided into two universes: the universe of development, wealth, prosperity, domination and power, and the universe of underdevelopment, misery, poverty, dependent, dominated and powerless peoples. We ask why this one is the universe of others, and why this one is our universe.[6]

Mveng reflected on the problems facing our word, our continent, with his African religious jacket. To understand this, means to see him as this African "son of the soil," this African religious, this artist, all at once, etc. He did this for the good of Africa, for our good, and not for his own glory.

Our part of the heritage

When someone goes get dead wood, he brings back the bundle he likes. The bundle brought by Mveng combined religious life in Africa, intellectual life, artistic life, to keep his identity as an African.

As an African Jesuit, Mveng worked to root the Gospel in Africa, notably through inculturation. For him, the African Christian must not lose his identity by moving away from his culture

---

5. Mveng and Lipawing, *Théologie, libération et cultures africaines*, 5.
6. Mveng, "Paupérisation et développement en Afrique," 111

and tradition. He must live this symbiosis of African identity and faith in the Gospel of Jesus Christ.

Two concerns seem major in the mvengian vision of the experience of the faith: the rooting and the conversion of civilizations.

The rooting

For Mveng, it is a duty for Africans who believe in the Good News of Jesus Christ to be fully Africans and Christians at the same time. For he says: "The loss of African identity is a danger for all humanity, because Africa has a role to play in the history of world civilization."[7] So we have to find our sources, our values.

The conversion of civilizations

The second concern is to convert civilizations. "The second challenge is that we have to convert. To become a Christian is not to become Westernized, it is to recognize that the message of Christ is addressed to all men. (. . .) Conversion obliges us to abandon or transform certain customs which go against our conscience. But our core values which the Gospel renews and enriches are not to be discarded."[8] Mveng did not advocate a divorce of cultures, but rather a universal marriage of cultures where everyone had to bring his share of richness. Being a Christian for him means therefore being a citizen of the world.

We have to reflect on ourselves, to see how we can, in our own way, be authentic Africans while becoming more universal.

Conclusion: "If you please God, men do not appreciate you too much."

Mveng had his limits and weaknesses. Some did appreciate him, others dit not. Probably for their own reasons. Moreover, isn't this

7. Mveng, *Pirogue*, 27.
8. Mveng, *Pirogue*, 27.

the case for all of us? Everyone knows that Mveng was murdered. By whom? Why? For what reason? There lies the enigma of the problem.

In an interview published by La Croix, Jean Marc Ela (a friend of Mveng, who died in exile in Canada in 2008) stated that: "These are mystical networks that eliminate intellectuals, people who disturb. Father Mveng was buried without his brain . . . The entire Cameroonian press said so. And we know that these mystical cults use human organs."[9]

However, investigations are continuing to find out the people behind this death . . . Criminals therefore remain to stare at. But until when? The question remains.

As Father Hebga said in his homily at Father Mveng's funeral: "Father Engelbert Mveng was above all a priest and companion of Jesus. This is the main thing. This is the key to his life."[10]

And we can add, if God is for Mveng, who will be against Mveng? Thank you.

9. Ela, La Croix, 12.
10. Hebga, *Nouvelles de la PAO*, 11.

Chapter Five

The XXIst Century

A Century of Anthropological De-pauperization of the Ntù?

> This last chapter is a meditative reflection made from a deliberately qualified exercise: "le regard regardé". In this exercise, Africa is questioned, is invited to look itself in the face. Therefore, a question arises. What does Africa do on its own? A spiritual and symbolic wash is proposed to wish the advent of another Africa. In this spiritual and symbolic wash, the question of the 21st century arises: a century of grace for Africa?

IN AFRICA, WHEN A woman is pregnant and ready to give birth, her family members or her spouse's family members ask themselves several questions to prepare for the birth of the baby : what sex will the child be? Who will he/she be? Will he/she be valiant as such an ancestor or not? Will he/she be a source of happiness for the family? In short, so many questions asked that find their answers, some from the birth of the child, others much later. Furthermore, the circumstances of the birth will determine the child's name.

Similarly, when it comes to preparing a party or welcoming an important guest, questions are raised, inherent in the character to be welcomed. To some extent, some guests are signs of misfortune, while others are signs of happiness,[1] depending on whether their arrival is followed or preceded by one or the other event.

What should we think about anthropological poverty, especially when it comes at starting a century (ours has been active for more than twenty years) during which painful events marked the previous century for our continent? Should we remain pessimistic or optimistic?

A new host has been there for more than twenty years: it did not ask for our opinion because its coming was necessary on its own. What will the 21st century be like in Africa and for Africa? What are the challenges and expectations ? These are all questions that Africans who are committed to changing the affairs of their many cities should ask themselves. But does it really depend on them?

"*Le regard regardé*"[2]: How does Africa look at itself?

It is not uncommon to note that with all the problems facing our continent, Africans are not happy with the way "city" affairs are managed. In general, they criticize certain experiences (most of them) and appreciate those that work. In short, they know and see that things overall are going badly.

Why in the past these wars in Somalia, DR Congo, Sierra Leone, Congo? Why these mutinies in the Central African Republic? Why these armed conflicts in Darfur, these terrorist acts in West Africa? Why so far do we continue to talk about underdevelopment and not poverty? Does Africa refuse development? Why

---

1. When a misfortune is preceded or followed by the visit of an important person, it is very likely that this person will be as a bad luck charm. A happy event, a good luck charm.

2. "Le regard regardé" is " a reflexive, self-critical exercise that any reasonable being can exercise on an object of his choice provided that this exercise is not complacent or vulgar, but just reasonable; fair, thinking and constructive. In short, an exercise that puts everyone before his own conscience and the conscience of an entire people". See H.-H. Kibangou, "Ecrire le Congo à partir d'une multitude de failles . . . ," 57.

do some African countries remain the preserve of certain foreign powers? All these questions, and others, are questions that lead Africa to look itself in the face and question itself.

Africa's view of itself is undoubtedly an interrogative look. A look that is half pessimistic and half optimistic. When will the promised land be ? At this pace, do you think things will move forward? But why do our leaders act disappointingly towards their peoples ? Why this selfishness on their part ? Why do we let them act selfishly? What are we doing to prevent them from doing so ? The answers to these questions are groping and mixed. Feelings are shared. Depending on the pace of events, we can move from optimism to pessimism, and vice versa. And yet, a wash with plenty of water is necessary.

The observation of the look : a wash with plenty of water

The washing in question is both corporeal and spiritual. In other words, it is symbolic. What to wash, why wash? Africans must wash everything that is dirty in them, everything that soils Africa. Because for too long, they were made to believe that they were worthless. Hence the animal treatment inflicted on them. And now between them, there are problems (and what problems!), wars, conflicts, hatred, jealousy, etc. We must wash everything to change mentalities, work hard to start hoping for another Africa.

The other Africa: Seeing Africa from another perspective

Africans are called to see things differently, to view Africa differently. For them it is a question of having noble and profound reasons to build the continent. To do this, they must make a great examination of conscience to see the whole journey made through past centuries. It goes without saying that great sacrifices are to be made. What is meant by this? It is a question of starting from new bases (based on what we have as our heritage), an African spirituality of development. To do this, we must start making an inventory of what we have as "possibilities to . . ." Why do we always seek to want what is above our possibilities? We have in our countries human potentialities, i.e., geniuses who "insignificantly" develop their countries because they are not followed and have no means to advance their countries at the national and international level; which is kind of miniature development. Wouldn't it be beneficial to allow all these little geniuses to develop their talents? (This is only an aspect certainly, but of real value). There are others, but should be addressed in order of priority. In several African countries, politicians or, better said, certain impolitical politicians do not know the notion of "priority." The question is how to understand, for example, that a government spends more than 27 billion FCFA to celebrate its 50th anniversary of the country's independence, when people do not have water or electricity? How is this possible?

Another thing, in Africa, the stars of "profession" in vogue (in the broad sense of the term) are almost unkown. These include, for example, musicians, soccer players or athletes in general, popular traders, etc. As for knowing the stars of the "not in vogue" professions, (and perhaps the most serious and priority ones), there is a whole problem that should be seriously considered. Where are the Roger Milla, Abedi Pele, George Weah, Gebre Selassie, Franco Luambo Makiadi, Youlou Mabiala, Pamelo Mounka, Yvonne Chaka Chaka, etc. of mecanics, carpentry, masonry? Where are the Eboussi Boulaga, Obenga, Anta Diop, etc. the Mveng of technology? Certainly, each of these professions requires a certain immediate audience (for soccer, because it is a game), but it is still an audience. However, in such a situation, politics and strategy are required.

Europe has not hesitated to push its geniuses far to prevent them from going unnoticed. Why wouldn't Africa do as much?

Africa, what do you do with your geniuses?

Africa, what do you do with your body and your limbs?

Africa, what do you do with yourself? Africa, what do you do with your wealth?

The XXIth Century : A Century of grace for Africa?

From all the above, it appears that the 21st century will be what Africa will do with it. It is our duty to provoke an earthquake at the level of thought, reflection, to allow this continent to maintain its own geniuses: the geniuses of its politics, development, economy, technology, etc. To all, when the hour of active grace arrives, we will say, "Go ahead, don't hesitate! Because, despite our problems, it is strictly forbidden not to have reason to hope. And as Axelle Kabou stated, we must "detoxify mentalities, set the record straight, and above all put individuals in front of their responsibilities."[3]

---

3. Axelle Kabou, Et si l'Afrique refusait le développement?, 27.

Conclusion

A Pertinently Philosophical Question

AT THE END OF this journey on anthropological pauperization, what should be said at best, what should be retained?

If there is one thing to remember, it is first and foremost this double dialogical dimension that ntù follows, through the Mvengian vision of anthropological pauperization. This double dimension is presented as follows:

1. The mvengian vision of the anthropological pauperization is this questioning of the ntù to the West, about his past condition, and whose consequences are manifested to the present day. But Engelbert Mveng does not stop there.

2. The second dimension is much more empowering, reflective, engaging and committed at the same time. This second dimension is no other than the questioning of the ntù about himself, about his own condition, here and now. This dimension is also a real manifestation of the ntù to want to change his fate into a chosen destiny. It is thus a real awareness of the ntù to want to change the course of his history. This historical change states Engelbert Mveng, must begin with a certain historical-cultural possession. What does it mean? The ntù must possess throughout history, his culture.

As Cheikh Anta Diop states, "What is important for science, for the progress of humanity, for the development and the

A Pertinently Philosophical Question

fulfillment of the consciousness of African peoples, is the recognition of the historical-cultural continuity."[1]

Can the allusion to a path for philosophical reflection be organized into philosophical knowledge? Relevant question to which an attempt to answer is possible, by more or less following the path of anthropological pauperization.

Identifying, in fact, the various detours of anthropological pauperization, such has been the path taken. A careful reading of this journey has shown that the mvengian vision of anthropological pauperization—if taken seriously— actually lays the groundwork for serious philosophical reflection. Before being the question of the State as an instrument of pauperization, anthropological pauperization is mainly the question of the ntù in search of his identity.

The ntù is the only subject of the African universe that has offered itself to this reflection; it is the intentional relationship of being-in-the-African world, the subject pole. The question of its existence is the question of the meaning and foundation of the meaning of human existence.

In this perspective, the ntù is a reflective subject, a thinking subject, here and elsewhere, now and always, with regard to the problematic (mentioned above) in which he is found.

The human being can only realize himself in the world (and in time), not because he is pure object, but because being a subjectivity, he can only express himself in relation to an objectivity.

In this sense, anthropological pauperization therefore appears as an original instrument that researchers, political scientists, philosophers, anthropologists, sociologists, African (and non-African) historians, will be able to use to examine the evil from which Africa suffers.

According to Tshiamalenga Ntumba,[2] four moments must determine appreciably, the goal set by any philosophy. As a first moment, there is thematic selection, followed by critical and

1. Diop, *Antériorité des civilisations nègres*, 74.

2. Tshiamalenga, "Les quatre moments de la recherche philosophique africaine aujourd'hui," 71–80.

faithful restitution, then historical reconstruction and finally, creation.

The thematic selection must allow the philosopher to make choices on very precise themes. This selection is accompanied by the choice of the angle from which the philosopher intends to approach his problematic.

As for the second moment (restitution), its attestation will be certified by the pre-existence of explicit texts.

Reconstruction (third moment), whatever it may be, "is a hermeneutic."

The fourth moment (creation) expects a dose of originality from African thinkers.

In the same perspective, Cheikh Anta Diop thinks that, to qualify a work (a thought) as philosophical or to see in it a path for an effective philosophy, two verification criteria are needed.[3]

1. It must be aware of itself, of its own existence, as a thought;
2. It must have achieved, to a sufficient degree, the separation of myth and concept.

These four moments, and these two criteria, were observed by Mveng. In this sense, it can be said that indeed, his vision of anthropological pauperization constitutes a path for philosophical reflection on the ntù.

Africa needs men of the stature of Engelbert Mveng, Cheikh Anta Diop or his disciple Théophile Obenga, and many others, to solve the problems specific to Africa. That is to say "lucid and fertile minds, capable of reaching effective solutions and being aware of them by themselves, without the slightest intellectual tutelage."[4]

The mvengian vision of anthropological pauperization can indeed be the object of an in-depth study in our universities, especially at St Pierre Canisius Faculty of Philosophy in Kinshasa (DR Congo), if it is admitted that these are places of culture and promotion of knowledge.

3. Anta Diop quoted by Ngoma Binda, *La philosophie africaine contemporaine*, 122.

4. Ela, *Cheikh Anta Diop ou l'honneur de penser*, 136.

A Pertinently Philosophical Question

Our hope is that, the mvengian vision of anthropological pauperization, will stimulate young African thinkers to research, and allow them to find effective solutions to our problems, to the problems of the African continent in particular, and the world in general.

Through this theory of anthropological pauperization, Mveng has brought a new, systematized and coherent teaching to the production of thought in Africa. And as Obenga states, "Any new teaching is necessarily an evidence of refusals, even daring and fervor. This is not illogical."[5]

---

5. Obenga, *Pour une nouvelle histoire*, 11.

Epilogue

Shortly before his assassination, Professor Engelbert Mveng organized a Symposium on Moses the African. The texts of this Colloquium were never published, for reasons that we ignore. We hope that they will be published one day! Not to mention his other writings that have not yet been published.

We also hope that one day, the Cameroonian political authorities will give this house to the Society of Jesus (Congregation to which Engelbert Mveng belonged) and will shed light on the death, O how tragic and violent, of this illustrious man of science.

Bibliography

Diop, Cheikh Anta. *Antériorité des Civilisations Nègres. Mythe ou vérité historique* ? Collection préhistoire/Antiquité Négro-africaine. Paris: Présence Africaine (2e édition), 1993.
Durozoi Gérard and André Roussel. *Dictionnaire de philosophie.* Paris: Ed. Nathan, 1990.
Eboussi Boulaga, Fabien. "Nous sommes victimes de ne pas oser penser." *Ivoire Dimanche* (681), 26/02/ 1984, 22–23.
———. "L'honneur de penser". In Terroirs 001, may (1992), 3.
Ela, Jean-Marc. *Cheikh Anta Diop ou l'honneur de penser.* Paris: L'Harmattan, 1989.
———. "Un culte satanique s'organise dans les allées du pouvoir". In La Croix, september 6 (1995), 12.
Elenga, Yvon Christian. "Engelbert Mveng (1930–1995): l'invention du discours théologique." *Hekima Review* (19) 91–104, May 1998.
Gusdorf, Georges. *Pourquoi des professeurs ?* Paris: Ed. Payot, 1963.
Hebga, Meinrad. "Eloge de l'ethnophilosophie". In Présence Africaine n°123 (1982): 20–41.
Jésuites. *Annuaire de la Compagnie de Jésus* 1974-1975. "Engelbert Mveng, sj. Province d'Afrique Occidentale." Rome: Ed. de la Curie Generalice, 1974.
Kabou, Axelle. *Et si l'Afrique refusait le développement ?* Paris: Ed. L'Harmattan, 1991.
Kibangou, H.-H. "Ecrire le Congo à partir d'une multitude de failles. Essai d'une grammaire de l'espérance sociale." In Cahiers du Gires (Groupe interdisciplinaire de recherches sur l'Eglise et la société). Les voies de l'espérance au Congo-Brazzaville (2020) : 55–76. Paris: L'Harmattan.
———. "Mveng et nous". First Mveng days at the Faculty of Philosophy St Pierre Canisius of Kimwenza/Kinshasa (DR Congo/academic year 1997-1998): 1–12. Non published
Labou Tansi, Sony. *La vie et demie.* Paris: Ed. du Seuil, 1979.
L'Effort camerounais number 22 (1019) from 28 April to 12 May 1995. Douala: L'Effort camerounais.

Bibliography

Mveng, Engelbert. *L'Afrique dans l'Eglise. Paroles d'un croyant.* Paris: L'Harmattan, 1985.

———. "Paupérisation et Développement en Afrique." *Terroirs* 001 (1992) 111–19.

Mveng, Engelbert and Benjamin Lipawing. *Théologie, Libération et Cultures Africaines. Dialogue sur l'anthropologie négro-africaine.* Yaoundé-Paris: Clé/Présence Africaine, 1996.

Ngoma, Binda. *La philosophie africaine contemporaine. Analyse historico-critique.* Recherches Philosophiques Africaines 21 (1994). Kinshasa-Limete: Facultés Catholiques de Kinshasa.

Nkeramihigo, Théoneste. *Initiation à l'acte philosophique.* Kinshasa-Limete: Ed. Loyola, 1991.

Nouvelles de la PAO. *L'assassinat du Père Mveng, sj. (1930–1995).* NPAO 137 (1995), 20 June 1995.

Ntima, Kanza. *Non. Je ne mourrai pas, je vivrai. Méditation sur le cheminement christologique en Afrique.* Kinshasa-Limete: Ed. Loyola, 1996.

Ntumba, Tshiamalenga. "Les quatre moments de la recherche philosophique africaine aujourd'hui." *Bulletin de Théologie Africaine* 5 (1981), vol. III, janvier-juin, 71–80.

Nzuzi, Bibaki. *Le Dieu-Mère. L'inculturation de la foi chez les Yombe.* Kinshasa-Limete: Ed. Loyola 1993.

Obenga, Théophile. *Pour une nouvelle histoire.* Paris: Ed. Présence africaine, 1980.

———. *L'Afrique dans l'Antiquité. Égypte pharaonique-Afrique.* Paris: Présence Africaine, 1973.

———. *La philosophie africaine de la période pharaonique. 2780–330 avant notre ère.* Paris: L'Harmattan, 1990.

Pirogue 75 (1989). Les Jésuites en Afrique. Abidjan: PAO.

Poucouta, Paulin. "Engelbert Mveng: une lecture africaine de la Bible." *Nouvelle Revue Théologique* 102 (1998), 32–45.

Prelot, Marcel. *La science politique.* Paris: PUF, 1963.

Rahner, Karl. *Theological investigations.* Volume II. London, Darton, Longman & Todd: Baltimore Helicon Press, 1962.

Sango Ya Kimwenza 19 (1995). Hommage au Père Engelbert Mveng), 15 May 1995. Kinshasa: Sango Ya Kimwenza.

Index

Action /actions, v, xiv, 20, 25, 33, 46
Abiding love, for Africa, xiii
Accumulation, of good materials, 9
Adults, 14
Africa, x, 6, 8, 13, 17, 29, 32, 34, 39, 40, 43, 47, 51, 52, 55, 58, 59
Africa, history of, 13
African archeology, 5
African christianity, 16
African continent, 17
African cultural context, 16
African history, 5
Africaninism, 28, 29
Africanitude, 28
African philosophical and theological reflection, 17
African political leaders, 10
African religious and intellectual world, 1
African poverty, 14
African/Africans, vi, ix, xiv, 32, 36, 37, 47, 48, 49, 51, 52, 53, 56, 57, 58, 61
African context, 15, 17
African continent, x, 5, 17, 46, 63
African culture, 4, 5, 8, 16
African man, ix, xv, 14, 16, 18, 19, 46
African men, xiii

African peasant, 27
African people, ix, 9, 61
African philosophy, ix, x, xiii, xv, xvi, 39, 40, 41, 42
African philosophizing, 45
African society /african societies, ix, x, 43, 44
African State, 9, 10, 11, 12, 23, 30, 32, 36, 43, 44, 45
African theology, of liberation, 6, 7
African thinkers, 62, 63
African traditions, 42
Africa's fragility, 15
African personality, 18
African women, xiii, 19
Alioun Diop museum, 4
Amougou, Jean, 2
Amougou, Jeanne, 4
Anthropological angle, 11, 12, 16, 17
Angles (anthropological, political, sociological), 11
Anthropological pauperization, theory of, x, xiv, xvii, 19, 42, 43, 63
Anthropological pauperization, x, xv, xvi, 1, 7, 10, 11, 13, 14, 15, 16, 17, 18, 19, 20, 22, 23, 24, 25, 26, 28, 29, 37, 38, 42, 43, 44, 45, 46, 60, 61, 62, 63

Index

Anthropology, 15, 16, 17, 18, 19, 22, 23, 24, 25
Apparatus, of pauperization, 10, 11
Anthropological annihilation, 13, 14, 15, 18, 29
anthropologists, 46, 61
AOTA (Ecumenical Associationn of African Theologians), 3
Approach, xiv, 6, 12, 42
Archeological research, 4
Aristotle, 24
Armies, 10
Article, 8, 11, 13, 19, 21, 44
Art, 3, 4, 5, 18, 50
Assimilation, 14
Assistance, 29, 33, 37
Author, xvi, 5, 20, 23, 39, 40, 48

Balafon, 5
Banal problems, xvi
Basins of Congo, 32
Being-there, xv
Beggar State, 12
Belgian Congo (Ex-Zaïre), 3
Bibaki, Nzuzi, xi, xiv, 5, 46
Biography, xvi, 2
Bible, 7
Black Africa, xiv, 9, 29,
Black man /Black African Man, 6, 10, 11, 13, 16, 20, 42
Black people, 14, 17
Black race, 13
Blondel, 20
Book, xiv, xv, xvi, xvii, 3, 13, 16, 19, 41, 42, 51
Broquette-Gonin prize, 3

Cameroon, 2, 3, 4, 5, 32
Cameroon's National pilgrimage office, 3
Cameroonian Jesuit, xvii, 3
CARI (African center for research on inculturation), 4
Capitalism, 17

Categories, 17
Central African Republic, 56
Century, xvii, 51, 55, 56, 57, 59
Chaka Chaka, Yvonne, 58
Children, 14, 31, 47
Civilization /Civilizations, 6, 48, 51, 53
Colonizer, 10, 11
Concept, xvi, 1, 7, 11, 16, 18, 19, 20, 26, 39, 62
Conditions of life, 27
Congo, 32, 56
Church of the Holy Angels (Chicago), 4
Colonial era, 14
Colonial powers, 14
Colonial rule, 16
Colonization, 13, 14, 15, 18, 29, 30, 31, 32
Conference / Conferences, 6, 20, 48
Congregation of the Beatitudes, 3
Collective awarness, 9
Commentary, xvi, 20
Commitment, xiii, 50
Competence, vi, xiii, xiv
Complacent / Complacency, xiv, 49, 56
Continent, ix, x, 1, 5, 17, 32, 40, 41, 44, 49, 51, 52, 56, 57, 59, 63
Contributions, xiv, xvi, 5, 6, 39, 43
Cooperation, 29
Countries/country, xv, 6, 8, 9, 13, 24, 27, 32, 34, 35, 37, 45, 51, 57, 58
Countries, of abundance, 9
Countries of the Third world, 9
Corruptive pauperization, 11, 12, 23, 34
Creation, 18, 62
Creative freedom, 16
Creative genius, 18
Creative thought, 17
Creativity, 16, 18

Index

Critical and faithful restitution, 61–62
Crisis, 8, 27, 28, 43, 52
Criteria, x, 62
Criticize, theory of, xvii
Cry, of despair, 8
Cultural axis, 6
Cultural advantages, 9
Cultural liberation, 46, 47
Cultural pauperization, 11, 12, 23, 36, 37
Culture, vi, ix, xiv, xv, 6, 16, 18, 19, 20, 42, 46, 51, 52, 53, 60, 62

Dakar, 4
Dasein, 20
Dead philosophy, x
Death, 17, 18, 28, 43, 45, 48, 49, 51, 54, 64
Debt, 35
Definition, 10, 19, 24, 26
Demanding, xiii, xiv
Democracy, 32
Democratic Republic of the Congo / DR Congo, xvi, 3, 56, 62
Determinism, 16
Destitution, state of, 17
Development of Africa and in Africa, xiv
Deep and abiding love for Africa, xiii
Defunct question, xiii
Department of History, 4
Dependence, 10, 12, 14, 27, 29, 33
Depersonalization, 16, 18
Deprivation, 9, 10
Descartes, xv
Desired destiny, ix, 27, 28, 38
Destiny, 6, 14, 26, 27, 60
Destiny, of the black peoples, 14
Director of Cultural Affairs of the Federal Republic of Cameroon, 4
Diggers, xiii

Dignity, 4, 13, 16, 18, 30, 33, 36
Dimensions, ix, x, 12, 25, 28, 46
Dictatorship, 34, 47
Diop, Cheikh, Anta, xiv, 47, 58, 60, 62
Djuma (Kwilu), 3
Domination, 10, 15, 16, 27, 29, 33, 52
Dominable, 28
Dominating ideology, 28
Douala, 3

Ebolowa, 2
Economic sovereignty, 10
Economist, 27
Eboussi, Boulaga, Fabien, xv, 8, 58
Economics, 15
Economy, 16, 59
Economic crisis, 8
Economic context, 16
Emblematic and prophetic figure, 1
Empires of West Africa, 32
Ends, xiii
Engelbert, 2
Earth, xvi, 24, 40
Ela, Jean-Marc, 54
Elenga, Yvon Christian, 5
Enam-Nkal of Minlaba, 2
Equatorial Guinea, 32
Ethnophilosophy, 44
Essence, 18, 27
Exclusivist way, of conceiving things, xvi
Existential crisis, 28
Exploitation, 13, 18
Extra-terrestrial, xvi
Ethnophilosophy, xv
Ethnotheology, xv
Exclusion, 9
Existence, xiii, xv
Existential ethics, xv, xvi
Experience, xv
Eurocentrisim, 32
Europe, xvi

Index

European, Asian, Oceanic or American philosophy, xv
Europeans, xiii
Ewondo, 2

Factors, 9
Faith, 17
False modesty, xiv
Families, 9, 14
Familiy tree, 31
Fight, 18
Figure, 30
Foreign powers, 10, 12
Fourvière (Lyon), 3
Fragility, 15
France, 3
Freedom, 9
French, 2
French Academy, 3

Gabon, 32
Geniuses, 59
God, 6, 7, 48, 50, 53
Greek, 2
Good direction, x
Good news, 15
Good-Samaritan State, 12
Gospel, 15, 52
Grassroots communities, 17
Gusdorf, George, 2

Hampâte Bâ, Amadou, 49
Hebga, Meinrad Pierre, 44, 54
Heidegger, xvii, 20
Hekima College, 4
Historical axis, 6
Historical angle, 12, 13, 14, 17
Historical reconstruction, 61
History, xiii, 2, 12, 14, 15, 16, 17, 18
Human dignity, 13
Human history, 15
Human misery, 15
Humanity, xiii, 8, 13

Human rights, 13

Identity, 17, 18
Ideology, 18
Ignorance, 26
Image, of God, 16
Imperialistic illusion, xvi
Impolitical politicians, 58
Inculturation, 4
Indigence, multiple, 12, 17
Indigenous, 17
Industry, 15
Injustice, 9, 26
Indebtedness pauperization/ pauperization of indebtedness, 11, 12, 35, 36
Independence, 9, 29
Individuals, 9
Individuality-collectivity, level, ix
Institutions, 9, 11
Instrument, 10
Instrument, of annihilation, 9
Instrument, of domination, 10
International solidarity, 29

Jerusalem, 3
Jesuits, xvi
Jesus Christ, 15
Journey, xvi

Kabou, Axelle, 35, 59
Kibangou, H-H, 46, 48
Kant, xvii
Kinshasa/DR Congo, xvii, 48
Kolvenbach, Peter Hans, 5

Ladrière, Jean, vi
Lack, of culture, xv
Lack, of a proper monetary system, 10
Lack, of a military power, 10
Lachelier, 2
Languages, 18
Latin, 2
Latin America, 13, 17

Index

Le Sillon, college, 4
L'Effort camerounais, 2
Legacy of colonization, 30
Le Monde, 3
Levels, 12
Liberation, 9, 18
Liberation, cultural, ix
Libermann College, 3
Library, 49
Lies, 26
Life, concept of, 17
Life, xvi
Linguistic abuse, xiii
Lipawing, Benjamin, xv, xvi, 16, 18
Lived experience, xvi
Luambo Makiadi, Franco, 58
Lourdes, 3

Mabiala, Youlou, 58
Major Seminary of Otele, 2
Man, xv
Manuals, xv
Marxism, 17
Mechanisms, 10, 12, 16, 17, 25, 33, 35
Mechanisms, of pauperization, 12, 16, 17
Mechanisms of impoverishment, 25
Meditation, 26
Meditative reflection, 55
Men, 14
MICA (Movement of African Catholic Intellectuals), 3
Mentality, level, x
Mental, x
Mercenaries, 31
Metaphysics, 45
Middle Ages, 13
Mimetala, 4
Milla, Roger, 58
Minor Seminary of Efok, 2
Minor Seminary of Akono, 2
Misery, 8, 15, 17, 27

Mission, 14
Money, 10
Mounka, Pamelo, 58
Mveng, Engelbert, x, xiv, xv, xvii, 1, 2, 3, 4, 5, 6, 7, 8, 9, 10, 11, 15, 16, 18, 19, 20, 26, 27, 28, 31, 32, 36, 38, 40, 43, 44, 46, 48, 49, 50, 51, 52, 53, 54, 58, 60, 61
Mveng days, xvi
Mvengian vision, of anthropological pauperization, x , 19, 60, 62
Mvengian thought, 6
Music, 2
Musicians, 58
Mvolyé, 4

Namur (Belgium), 3
Negro art museum, 4
Negro african philosophy, 40
Ngoma Binda, 34
Ngoro, 4
Nkol Afeme, xvii
North America, 13
Noumenal asphyxia, 28
Noviciate of the Society of Jesus, 2—3
Ntolo, Barbe, 2
Know-how, xiii
National Commission for Ecclesiastical History of Cameroon, 3
Negro Arts Festival, 4
Ntù, ix, x, xiv, xv, xvi, 6, 7, 10, 11, 19, 20, 22, 23, 24, 25, 26, 27, 28, 29, 30, 31, 32, 33, 34, 35, 36, 37, 38, 39, 42, 43, 45, 46, 47, 55, 60, 61, 62
Ntù being, x, 26, 27
Ntù people, 25

Obenga, Théophile, xv, 40, 41, 42, 58, 62, 63
Ojectivity, 61

Index

Old-fashioned story, xiii
Old people, 14
Obobogo, 4
Onomasiology, 26
Opinion, xiv, 9, 10, 20, 26, 56
Oppression, 10, 11, 16, 26, 37, 47
Oppressor / Oppressors, 11, 31
Originality, 18

Particular attention, xiv
Palaver, model of democracy, 32
Pauperization, 10, 11, 12, 16, 18, 25, 26, 28, 30, 31, 33, 35, 36, 38, 43, 44, 46
Pauperization of indebtedness, 11, 12, 23, 35, 36
Pele, Abedi, 58
People / peoples, ix, xiv, xvi, 6, 8, 8, 10, 11, 14, 15, 17, 18, 27, 32, 34, 35, 44, 46, 49, 50, 52, 54, 56, 57, 58
Personal ethics, xv, xvi, 38
Phenomenon, 9
Phenomenon asphyxia, 28
Philantropic apparatus, of domination, 29
Philosophical system, 26
Philosophy, ix, x, xiii, xv, xvi, 2, 3, 18, 19, 20, 23, 24, 39, 40, 41, 42, 44, 45, 46, 61, 62
Philosophy of Eboussi, of Tshiamalenga, of Obenga, of Hountondji, xv
Philosophies, xv
Philosophy of Descartes, Kant or Heidegger, xv
Philosophy of pauperization, 44
Philosophical production, ix, 19
Philosophical reflection, xiv, 19, 43, 45, 61, 62
Philosophical research, x, 43
Philosophical question, xv, 26, 27, 60
Placide Tempels, 40, 42
Plan, xv, xvi

Politics, 12, 15, 16, 17, 18, 24, 45, 58, 59
Political, ix, xiii, xv, 9, 10, 11, 12, 13, 14, 15, 16, 17, 24, 25, 43, 44, 45, 46, 61, 64
Political context, 16
Post-colonial Africa, 17
Post colonial african state, 10, 30, 43, 44, 45
Poor, the, 14, 47, 52
Poor countries, 27
Poucouta, Paulin, 5, 7
Poverty, 8, 9, 12, 14, 25, 27, 29, 45, 52, 56
Power / Powers, 9, 10, 12, 14, 27, 35, 43, 51, 52, 57
Powerful, the, 14
Powerless people, 27, 52
Priest, 2, 3, 49, 54
Price, xiv
Problem / Problems, ix, x, xv, xvi, 7, 10, 24, 26
problematic, xv, 27, 28, 30, 35, 38, 42, 61
problematic situation, 7, 22, 26,
prosperity, 27, 52
Province of Central Africa, 3
Pseudo-philanthropic pauperization, 11, 12, 33, 34

Questions, xv, 15, 23, 24, 27, 38, 55, 56, 57
Questioning, xv, xvi, 20, 22, 28, 60

Racial ideology, 14
Racial discrimination, 17
Racism, 15
Rahner, Karl, xv
Reagan, Ronald, 8
Reason / Reasons, xiii, 10, 2, 10, 27, 41, 49, 53, 54, 56, 57, 59, 64
Recognition, 9, 61
« Regard regardé », 55, 56
Relevance, 26, 28, 39, 42, 44

Index

Religion / Religions, 12, 14, 15, 16, 17, 18, 37
Religious angle, 13
Renard, Alain, 5
Reflexive advance, x
Reflection, xiv, xv, xvii, 7, 11, 13, 17, 19, 30, 32, 35, 48, 51, 59, 61
Reflecting, xv, xvi, 19, 49, 51
Rehabilitation, 16, 19
Religious experience, 7
Revalorisation, of African culture, 16
Rich, the, 14, 52
Rich countries, 8, 27, 45
Rights, 9, 16, 18, 24, 30
Rome, 3

Sédar Senghor, Léopold, 4
Selassie, Gebre, 58
Scientific research, 26
Self-liberation, 16
Selfishness, 27, 57
Service, of Africa, xiii
Scientific production, xvi
Sierra Leone, 56
Single people, xvi, 14
Skeleton, xiii
Slave trade, 13
Slavery, 29, 36
Subject, 61
Social animal, 25
Soccer players, 58
Social level, ix
Sociological angle, 11, 13, 17
Social and cultural advantages, 9
Social disengagement, 26
Social, ix, xv, 9, 14, 24, 25, 26, 35
Social reality, 24, 25
Sociologists, 46, 61
Sociology, 14, 15, 17, 24
Society of Jesus, 3, 64
Somalia, 56
Son of Africa, xiv
Sony Labou Tansi, 31

Spiritual emptiness, 15
Spiritual experience, 16
Spiritual and symbolic wash, 55
Spirituality, 7, 18
South Africa, 13
Sovereignty, 9, 10, 12, 32
State, 9, 10, 11, 12, 17, 22, 24, 25, 26, 29, 30, 32, 33
State, of indigeneity, 17
Story, xiii
Structure, 8, 9, 24, 29, 30
Structural pauperization, 11, 12, 15, 23, 29, 30, 31, 32, 38
Subject ntù, 30
Sub-Saharan Africa, 36
Subsistence system, based on absolute dependence, 10
Subsistence, 12
State of being, 22, 25
System, 14, 15, 18, 28, 29, 31, 34, 35
System, of domination, 15
St Francis Xavier community, 4
St Peter Canisius Faculty of Philosophy, xvi, 62

Technology, 58, 59
Thematic selection, 61, 62
Thinker / Thinkers, xiii, 2, 6, 39, 41, 44, 62, 63
Thinking, xiii, xvi, 50, 51, 56, 61
Theology, xv, 3, 18, 19
Theology-spirituality axis, 6
Third world, 8, 9, 12, 27
Thoughts, xiii, 39
Tshiamalenga Ntumba, 41, 61
Traditions, 18, 40, 42
Truth, xiii, xiv, 6, 8, 39, 40
Tyranny, 14

UNESCO expert consultant, 3
Universes, 27, 52
Union of Black World Writers, 4
Uniqueness, 18
United States, 8

Index

University of Yaoundé, 3, 4
Van Effenterre, Henri, 3
Victims, 15, 37, 47
« Vie et demie », 31
Vital, dimension / dimensions, x, 46

Ways, 50
Weak, the, 14
Wealth, 8, 27, 34, 36, 51, 52, 58
Weakness / weaknesses, 20, 44, 53
West Africa, 32, 56
Weah, George, 58
White, 30, 31
West African Province (AOC), xi, xvii
Western imperialism, 32
Woman / women, xiii, 6, 7, 19, 14, 48, 55

World, xv, 1, 5, 6, 8, 13, 16, 18, 19, 20, 26, 27, 33, 36, 46, 48, 51, 52, 53, 61, 63
Work, v, xi, xiii, xvi, xvii, 1, 4, 5, 7, 13, 15, 16, 19, 20, 23, 35, 40, 41, 42, 49, 50, 62
Writings, xvi, 1, 5, 7, 19, 20, 21, 40, 42, 44, 50, 64

Yaounde, xvii, 2, 4
Yaounde Cathedral, 4
Young people, 14

Zambezi, 32
Zoon politikon, 25